TRAVEL IN ENGLAND

1　The Mail-Coach Driver of 1832

From a print by Henry Alken

TRAVEL IN ENGLAND

FROM PILGRIM AND PACK-HORSE
TO CAR AND PLANE

By

THOMAS BURKE

Let him that purposeth to travell, first
Begin where he was born, bred up and nurst,
That's his own country.

A Survey of 26 Counties (1634)

B. T. BATSFORD LTD.

LONDON   -   NEW YORK   -   TORONTO   -   SYDNEY

Books by THOMAS BURKE

ENGLISH NIGHT-LIFE
THE STREETS OF LONDON
THE ENGLISH TOWNSMAN
THE ENGLISH INN
LIVING IN BLOOMSBURY
Etc.

First published, Autumn, 1942
Reprinted Edition, Winter, 1945–6
Reprinted, 1949

MADE AND PRINTED IN GREAT BRITAIN BY
JARROLD AND SONS LTD., NORWICH FOR
THE PUBLISHERS, B. T. BATSFORD LTD.,
LONDON: 15 NORTH AUDLEY STREET, W.I.
AND MALVERN WELLS, WORCESTERSHIRE,
NEW YORK: 122 EAST 55TH STREET.
TORONTO: 480-6 UNIVERSITY AVENUE.
SYDNEY: 156 CASTLEREAGH STREET.

Contents

Acknowledgment

As IN the other books in this Series, the publishers are heavily indebted to Messrs. Walter T. Spencer, of New Oxford Street, for the loan of many of the prints and drawings included among the illustrations. Of the photographs, fig. 16 is by E. Allen, St. Neots; fig. 93, by Bill Brandt; figs. 2, 3, 4, 5, 6 and 17, by the late Brian C. Clayton; fig. 18, by J. Dixon-Scott; figs. 21, 84, 88 and 90, by Dorien Leigh Ltd.; fig. 91, by General Photographic Agency; fig. 87, by Gibson & Sons, Penzance; and fig. 92, by courtesy of Rolls-Royce, Ltd. The remaining subjects are mostly from the author's and publishers' collections.

CHAPTER ONE

Making Tracks

WHEN THE early Britons first moved from homestead and settlement to see what was on the other side of the hill, and whether they could exchange their surplus goods with other settlements, the story of English travel began.

Of that beginning we have no record. Oblivion has scattered her poppy upon those adventurers, and their doings are buried in the darkness of the unknown past. A few relics of utensils and of objects of barter are all that remain for the building of conjecture. But from the tracks they made in their first movements across the wild land and the hills, grew the mighty roads and the surge of travel of to-day. When the first wanderers went in a band to find new settlements, and others followed in their steps, the first track was made; and from the trodden track grew the clear pathway from hamlet to hamlet, and to the coast; and from the pathway, the road; and with it, slowly but always increasing, a volume of movement across the face of the country, and the intercourse of man and man, and the exchange of goods and of ideas and legends.

Up and down those roads to-day, through every hour of the seven days, flows a constant stream of traffic—cars, motor-coaches, lorries, horse-vans, marching troops, tanks and guns; up and down those same roads which, for nearly twenty centuries, from their earliest days as tracks, have gleamed and twinkled with the paraphernalia of transport and travel. Along them have moved the chariots of the early British, and the helmets of the legions of Rome; companies of horse and of armoured knights and squires; litters, whirlicotes, Royal coaches, carriers' carts, lumbering stage-waggons, gigs, barouches, post-chaises, and brilliant mail-coaches. Pilgrims and pardoners have plodded along them, as secular pilgrims of to-day, with knapsack and rucksack, still plod along them. Drovers with their flocks and herds have crawled along them. Fugitives have fled along them. Sumpters, with their pack-horse trains, have struggled along them, against wind and storm, as their successors of to-day, the commercial representatives, buzz along them in their light cars.

Nothing greatly changes. The stream of life goes on always as one. The drops that make the stream pass on, but the stream is still there. The pageant of the English road has changed only in costume appurtenance, and the idiom of the travellers' speech. Otherwise, it is a company of similar men with similar hopes, fears, ambitions, ardours, mean desires, and noble purposes. Even the perils of the road have not lessened; with civilisation, they have indeed increased. Travellers in the earliest days knew the peril of losing their way, of sinking into a bog, of being snow-bound, of meeting with outlaws and robbers and vicious animals; they knew the peril of flooded roads, broken bridges, and treacherous guides. But in our own time greater numbers of people meet death on the road than ever met it in the days of unkempt roads and lawlessness; not only because more people travel, but because our perfected roads are thronged with things more deadly than wild animals or starving or bloodthirsty outlaws.

Travel to-day has many purposes and motives. But in the very early days, the young pioneer who first made a way across hill and moor and marsh, left home with one idea—to see the world and find fortune; and at that time he might trudge only twenty miles, to the settlement over the hill, and find a quite new world of different people with different ways of life, different speech, different appliances, and different gods. The excitement of travel was then a reality. Travellers of to-day know where they are going, and they know by their friends' talk, or by reading, something of the place they are going to, and what they will find there. But in those shadowy times there was nothing trustworthy to guide the adventurer; nothing beyond vague rumour or legend uttered in accents of wonder over the peat fire on the hut's floor. The unexpected was to be found at every bend of the road, every angle of the hill. Boarding a plane outside London and landing at Manchester in a matter of minutes provides something of a thrill; it can be nothing to the succession of thrills experienced by the traveller in the Britain of pre-Roman times.

Where to-day there are roads there were fens and swamps. Where is now a town was a dense wood. That is why most of the early tracks and bridle-paths go over hills or along the sides of hills (ridgeways) and why they make so many deviations. The first travellers kept to the hills not only to avoid ambush from above, but to avoid unfordable rivers, flooded fields, and impenetrable thickets. The winding tracks and roads of England were first trodden out in the days when all land was common, and when travellers, coming to a patch of swamp, struck a way round it. The journeys of most of those pioneers were pedestrian, since the foot of man could often go not only where the primitive cart could not go, but even where a horse or mule could not go.

When the Romans made their roads across and along the face of

2 A Prehistoric Artery: the Ridgeway Crossing the Berkshire Downs

3 A Prehistoric Green Track

4 A Roman Artery: Ermine Street passing through Lincolnshire

5 Roman Road Paving
in Dean Forest

6 Roman steps through
Hill Country

the country, they developed many of them from those early British tracks, but so far as possible they avoided mountains. They sought the straightest way between two points, and where the track went over a mountain, or was cut on its side, they mostly avoided it by a series of straight diagonal diversions, or cut through it. The chief of their roads were those known in later years as the Icknield Way (Gloucester to Norfolk); the Watling Street (Dover to Chester); the Fosse Way (Exeter to Lincoln); the Ermine Street (London to Lincoln and York); and Akeman Street (London to Bath). Most of these ways already existed, and when the Romans re-made them, mainly as military roads, they re-made them with such skill that sections of them are in use to this day. No such roads were to be made in England again until the appearance, in the nineteenth century, of Thomas Telford and John Macadam. The Romans made their roads with several layers of material, so that they could bear any burden of traffic. The surface of most of them was stone paving, and some of them were grooved to give extra speed to chariots and waggons. At intervals along each road they set millaria (or milestones), some of which are still preserved; mansiones (or posting-stations) forerunners of the inn; and stations (or towns). Under other names, many of those stations are the populous towns of to-day.

When, about the fifth century, domestic trouble drew the Romans away from Britain, civilisation lapsed, and free intercourse between distant parts almost ceased. During the occupation, the British had acquired the habit of letting the invader do things, with the result that when the invader had gone, and a new invader arrived from the north, the British were helpless. They could only try appease-ment on the new invader, or hire the help of outsiders who, having given the help, themselves became invaders. In this state of things, the Roman stations were destroyed, or left to decay, and the roads they had built were neglected until accumulations of soil buried them, and they disappeared many feet below the surrounding surface, or became grass-grown and obliterated. The darkness descended, and stayed for some centuries. Even the Normans, who were a little more advanced than the Saxons, did nothing, when they arrived, to improve the means of communication; and outside the towns the country relapsed into a wild state, with civilisation, if the term is not too extravagant, represented only by the fortress-castle.

But at last the long night ended, and a glimmer of daylight illuminated men's minds. Under the Plantagenets, disturbed as the country was, intercourse was again possible. Bridges were restored, and new roads were made. As the Romans followed roughly the old

B

British trackways, so those new roads followed those sections of the Roman roads which were still practicable. But there was no government supervision, no national system of roads, and there was to be none for several hundred years. That there were roads and bridges at that time at all is one of the few credits that can be given to the Church. It was the Church that took in hand the welfare of travellers, by the making and upkeep of roads and resting-places, and by serving them in other material ways, as with refreshment, and in spiritual ways by prayers for their safety. Men who were willing to help in the making or repair of roads and bridges, either by manual labour or by gifts of money, were given special religious indulgences and absolutions. Priests or lay hermits sat at the sides of the principal roads, collecting alms towards the good work. Every abbey received travellers as its guests, and while the wealthy made some payment, the poor were given free hospitality and helped on their way. Through centuries of years the Hospital of St. Cross, near Winchester, founded in the twelfth century, has, up to our own time, handed out, to all who ask, the Wayfarer's Dole—a piece of bread and a cup of "small beer."

Not until the fourteenth century do we find any records of, or more than a few references, to the experiences and doings of travellers over England. From the Rolls of Parliament and various Church papers we learn a good deal about the roads and bridges, their direction and construction and maintenance, but scarcely anything about the people who went up and down them. Official documents are all very well, but they never change their hue. We know them. Whether they are of the eleventh century or the twentieth, blue book is the fit name for them. The official mind is always the official mind, always of one cast; and never is the official report touched by the breath of life, or the warmth of the human hand, such as we get from personal diaries or records of day-to-day homely detail. Those records are more enlightening of a period than a hundred State documents. They take us at once into their atmosphere, so that we catch the very tang of the times, the very accent of the speech, the very odour of the food; and what is called the dead past—which, in official documents, it certainly is—becomes more alive than our own present.

But, as I say, before the fourteenth century, we have scarcely anything but sterile State papers. Then we begin to perceive a stir and the ordinary man comes to life and is heard to talk. We see him on his travels; business travels, private visits, pilgrimages. We see the coloured procession of all ranks and callings. We see the Royal Progress, with its attendant train of officers of the household, knights, esquires, bowmen, chamberlain, seneschal, cooks, lackeys—all of

whom had to be housed and fed by the lords of the different districts
through which the Progress passed. The Royal Progress was made
not only for the purpose of letting the people see their monarch,
and present their petitions, and receive boons or the rough edge of
justice; it was, for the monarch, a cheap way of living.

The great lords themselves were also in constant movement. The
estates of most of them were not set in one county; they were widely
scattered; and for purposes of economy, as well as to keep an eye on
things, their owners lived now at one, now at the other. When one

An English Carriage of the Fourteenth Century

castle's winter store of dried or salted foods was exhausted, they and
their retinue moved to the next. Winter was spent at their southern
estates, and the warmer months at their northern; so that the roads
were continually alive with their trains, which were only less
magnificent than a Royal Progress.

The conveyances of that time were of the rough and ready kind.
The monarch went on horseback. If his queen and women of the
court were travelling with him, they mostly used the same means,
riding either astride or on a pillion saddle behind a lackey; until,
towards the end of the century, the side-saddle was introduced. But
sometimes, for dignity, they rode in a primitive carriage—a huge,
lumbering, gilded vehicle, three times the size of the waggon of to-day.
Behind the Royal figures and their bodyguard, followed a train of
unwieldy carts, drawn by horses, oxen, or mules, carrying the Royal
baggage. When extra carts were required, they were commandeered
from neighbouring farmers or travelling merchants, who could go
and recover them wherever they might be discarded. For those who
fell sick on the way, or were injured, the horse-litter was used. This
was a contraption like a large sedan-chair, slung on long poles and
borne between two horses, driven tandem, with the front poles
strapped to the saddle of the leading horse, and the rear poles to the
collar of the second horse.

We see on the road, too, the judges on their circuits, booted and spurred, and the plodding foot-travellers—the minstrels, pedlars, jugglers, and hot-footed messengers claiming right of way over all. On the hills we see the pack-horse train, moving to the jingling of the bells which were hung on the leader's harness to warn other trains of its approach. All who were on the road had a reason for being there; no man travelled except by necessity, and none were on the road, intentionally, by night. Each man tried to time his journey

A Professional Messenger of the Fourteenth Century

to be actually a *journey*—*i.e.* a day's travel—so that at dusk he should be near shelter. In some forest districts—and a very large part of England was then forest—bells were rung at dusk in the neighbouring towns, as a warning that the gates would soon be closed, and as a guide to any who had missed their way. For those actually benighted, beacons were lit; here and there about the country one may still see churches carrying on their towers the cresset or fire-pot. Travellers who had been guided to safety by bells or beacons sometimes, in their wills, made bequests to ensure the continuance of the practice for future travellers. In certain parishes of Lincolnshire, Nottingham-shire, and Yorkshire, the terms of those bequests have been observed every night through all succeeding years—until suspended by war regulations.

So hazardous was travel considered that the Litany had a special clause for travellers. The danger at night was not only that of robbery and perhaps murder; there was the danger that, even with a lantern, one might take a few steps from the beaten track and be drowned, or plunge headlong to a hundred-feet drop. There was, of course, danger by day as well as night. The country was then so infested by robbers that all owners of land that bordered on frequented roads were commanded to cut away all bushes or other growth, behind which robbers might hide, to within two hundred feet of the road on either side. The robbers of that time were not only of the outlaw or vagabond kind. Some of the most noble barons were not above doing a bit of plunder. The fortunes of many a high and puissant family were founded in this way, on the robbery or holding to ransom of rich travellers. The barons would send out bands of their knights who would waylay drovers with their herds, merchants with their

A Medieval Chapman

goods, private travellers with their cart-loads of family possessions and gold, and seize the lot. Even if the traveller had nothing, he was often, if he looked like a man of substance, seized and confined in the castle until ransomed. Foot travellers and other poor people were rounded up and held as serfs for land labour. Any who resisted were killed.

Nobody, therefore, if he could help it, travelled alone. He waited until he could make one of a company. The only men who were safe in travelling alone were men of the Church. And so we have the pack-horse train, the company of merchants, the company of men travelling to the same place, and the company of pilgrims. The transport of goods was almost entirely by the pack-horse. It was a feature of the roads almost up to the nineteenth century, and we find memorials of it in the number of inns off the main roads bearing the sign of the *Packhorse* or the *Woolpack*. Other links, found in various lonely parts of the country, are the pack-horse bridges over streams—narrow and steeply arched, and with very low parapets so that the hanging pack shall not be dislodged. Goods of greater bulk were carried in a train of waggons.

A picture of the waggon-train of the western cloth-weavers is given in one of the "novels" of that earliest of novelists, Thomas Deloney. He was writing in the late sixteenth century, but his story is concerned with an earlier period, when the clothiers of the West of England and of East Anglia were making and exporting much cloth.

He shows the king of the time on the western road out of London meeting a number of cloth-wains, and, because of the narrow road, being forced to halt and pull to one side to let them pass. They numbered over two hundred. Nobody recognised him as king, and he was kept waiting for passage nearly an hour. Beginning to lose his temper, he demanded whose wains they were:

> The Waine-men answered in this sort: Colès of Reading (quoth they). Then by and by the King asked another, saying: Whose cloth is this? Old Coles (quoth he). And again anon after he asked the same question to others, and still they answered Old Coles. . . . Breaking out in discontent, by reason of his stay, he said, he thought Old Cole had got a commission for all the carts in the country to carry his cloth.

At Staines he met another company of carts filled with cloth, and asked in admiration whose *they* were; and was told:

> They be goodman Suttons of Salisbury, good sir; and by that time a score of them were past, he asked again, saying: Whose are these? Suttons of Salisbury (quoth they) and so still, as often as the King asked that question, they answered Suttons of Salisbury. God send me many such Suttons (said the King). And thus the farther he travelled westward, more wains and more he met continually; upon which occasion he said to his Nobles, That it would never grieve a King to die for the defence of a fertile country and faithful subjects. I always thought (quoth he) that Englands valour was more than her wealth, yet now I see her wealth sufficient to maintain her valour, which I will seek to cherish in all I may. . . .

In a succeeding chapter, two or three companies of merchants, with their trains, meet at Reading, and we see the manner in which men of those days took their ease at their inn:

> When Gray of Gloucester, and William of Worcester were come to Reading, according to their custom, they always called old Cole to have his company to London, who also duly attended their coming, having provided a good breakfast for them: and when they had well refreshed themselves, they took their horses and rode on towards the city. . . . Casting their eyes aside, they espied Tom Dove with the rest of his companions come riding to meet them, who as soon as they were come thither, fell into such pleasant discourses as did shorten the long way they had to Colebrook, where always at their coming towards London they dined; and being once entered into their inn, according to old custom, good cheer

The Pilgrims' Inn at Glastonbury (now the "George")

was provided for them; for these clothiers were the chiefest guests that travelled along the way; and this was as sure as an Act of Parliament that Tom Dove could not digest his meat without music, nor drink wine without women, so that his hostess being a merrie wench, would oftentimes call in two or three of her neighbours wives to keep him company; where, ere they parted, they were made as pleasant as Pies. . . . Tom Dove called for music, William of Worcester for wine, Sutton set his delight in hearing merry tales, Simon of Southampton got him into the kitchen, and to the pottage pot he goes, for he esteemed more a messe of pottage than of a venison pastie. Now sir, Cuthbert of Kendal was of another mind, for no meat pleased him so well as mutton, such as was laced in a red petticoat.

The pilgrimage to the shrine of a saint—to Walsingham, St. Edmundsbury, Glastonbury, Malmesbury, Durham, St. Albans, Canterbury—was then as regular an event of the year as the spring holiday of to-day. Mostly those pilgrimages were undertaken in all sincerity, but the journey itself was an occasion for jollification. It is to those pilgrimages that we owe the oldest of our inns, which began as the monastic hostel or the *maison dieu*, sometimes on the actual Way, and sometimes on the outer side of the gates of the towns. Among those still surviving are the George, at Glastonbury; the New Inn, at Gloucester; the Pilgrims' Hostel, at Battle; the George, at Winchcombe; the Hostel of God-Begot, at Winchester; the Seven Stars, at Alfriston; and the Falstaff, at the gate of Canterbury.

In official records we find many references to Pilgrims and Pilgrimages, but, happily for us, there was one who observed them with something warmer than the eye of the reporter, and out of them created one Pilgrimage which has been in progress for nearly six hundred years. The road between Dover and London is thronged with ghosts, but the most famous are not the ghosts of actual figures of history. They are that company of imagined (and therefore more real) people who are for ever on that road; who have never, like mortals, known bodily life and passed from it into the dark ice of death, but are preserved in the vital warmth of their creator's imagination. There they go—the Friar, the Man of Law, the Pardoner, the Merchant, the Innkeeper, the Franklin (small landowner), the Miller, the Reeve (bailiff), the Prioress, the Sumnor (officer of the Church), the Manciple (provisioner for colleges), the Knight, and the Wife of Bath. We see them in movement, we see them halting at ale-houses, and, above all, we hear their talk and their laughter.

In their company we have a crystallisation of the English life of the period; all social grades and all types of character are represented.

7   Medieval Pilgrims

8   A Fifteenth-Century Cavalcade

9 A Medieval Beggar

10 A Medieval Foot Traveller

11 A Two-wheeled Baggage Cart

As William Langland, on a May morning, dreams on his Malvern Hills and shows us, in the Vision of the Field Full of Folk, the abuses of the time, Chaucer balances the picture by showing us, in another May-time, the merriment of ordinary people and their joy in simple things. Down the road they go in an everlasting spring, with jest and story, and no doubt such songs as *Betuene Mershe and Averil*, or *I Know a Bird in Bower Bright*.

Nobody, as I say, travelled purely for pleasure, and the bulk of the traffic on the roads was that of the manufacturers and traders. At that time an important factor of trade-life was the Fair. Almost every town held at least two Fairs in the course of the year, and every Fair drew buyers and sellers and entertainers from all parts of the surrounding district. At the Fair the people from remote country hamlets laid in their year's stock of clothes and household goods, the farmers exchanged their cattle and their produce, and the makers of gauds and trifles found a custom they could only otherwise find by going from village to village. The most famous Fairs of that time were those held at Winchester, Weyhill, Cambridge (the Stourbridge Fair), Bristol, Nottingham, and Smithfield—Bartholomew's. Where-ever there was a Fair, the roads leading to that place were, for some days before its opening, filled with travellers—merchants with cloth-wains or pack-horses, pedlars, country housewives, farmers, servants offering themselves for a year's hire, quacks, tumblers, and beggars; and the inns and ale-houses on those roads were humming with life, and the inns of the town itself were overflowing.

The roadside inns were of a primitive kind, and were frequented neither by the noble, who preferred the hospitality of the nearest abbey or of some local lord; nor by the poor, who could not afford them. They were used mainly by the intermediate class—the mer-chant, the scholar, the husbandman, the chapman. The accommo-dation was mostly one or two rooms strewn with rushes, on which were laid a number of pallets. There were no separate bedrooms, and at that time no "ordinary." Each guest either brought his food with him or gave his own order for what the house could supply. The ale-houses or "ale-stakes" were just cottages or huts, usually kept by widows, and distinguished from their neighbours by nothing more than a pole bearing a few leafy boughs. It was on this, the earliest inn-sign, that the old proverb was based—Good wine needs no bush.

A constant figure on the roads, not only at Fair-time, but at all times, was the wandering minstrel or glee-man. Rahere, founder of Bartholomew's Hospital, was one. The minstrel not only attended

c

all public functions: he was welcome at almost any castle or great
house as an after-dinner or supper-time entertainer. In return for
such "lays" as *Guy of Warwick* or *Sir Bevis of Southampton*, he would
receive food and a night's lodging and various gifts in kind and money.
When he celebrated in song the prowess of the lord whose guest he
was, the gift was proportionately larger; and one may guess that he
made a point of learning something about the owner of each castle
he approached, so that some personal and flattering allusion could
be worked into his song.

A little pageant of the common figures of the road of that day,
similar to that presented by Chaucer, is presented in the Prologue to
The Vision Concerning Piers the Plowman—Skeat's version:

> Some choose to be chapmen, to chaffer for gain;
> And it seems to our sight, such surely succeed.
> And some, to make merry, as minstrels are wont,
> Getting gold with their glee, yet guiltless, I trust.
> As for jugglers and jesters, all Judas' children,
> That feign silly faces, apparelled as fools,
> Having wit, if they willed it, to work as they ought—
> I pass o'er what Paul would have preached of these sinners. . . .
>
> Next beggars and bedesmen were hustling about,
> Their bags and their bellies with bread were well cramm'd,
> By falsehood they fed them, and fought o'er their ale,
> As greedy as gluttons they go to their beds,
> And rise up as ribalds, these robber-like knaves. . . .
>
> Next pilgrims and palmers would plight them together
> To seek out Saint James and saints known in Rome;
> They went on their way with many wise tales,
> And had leave to tell lies all their lifetime after. . . .
> Of hermits a huge heap, with hooks to their staves,
> To Walsingham went; and their wenches went after;
> Great lubbers and long, that to labour were loath. . . .

The palmer was a sort of professional pilgrim. He did not journey
to one shrine to seek pardon for the year's misdeeds. He went from
one to the other, begging his keep on the way, and collecting souvenirs
from each shrine as proof of his pious journeys. Later in his poem,
Langland gives a vivid sketch of the type:

> He bare him a staff with a broad strip bound,
> That round it was twined like a woodbine's twist;
> A bowl and a bag he bare by his side;
> A hundred of vials was set on his hat,
> Signs from Sinai, Gallician shells;
> With crosses on his cloak, and the keys of Rome,
> And the vernicle before, that men should discern
> And see by his signs what shrines he had sought.

12   A Medieval Carriage   13   A Medieval Litter

14   Riding Pillion   15   A Pardoner

16 A Medieval Chapel on a Bridge: St. Ives, Huntingdonshire

17 A Medieval Packhorse Bridge: Bakewell, Derbyshire

Another constant figure of the roads was the messenger, the equivalent at that time of the postman. There were Royal messengers and private messengers. Each Court official had his own messengers, and the Church, the judges, and the great lords kept a staff of them. They were the swiftest travellers on the road: some of them could do the journey between London and Scotland in six days. They claimed precedence over all other travellers, and penalties were heavy for impeding them, or refusing them help in the way of fresh horses or short-cuts over private land. They could compel the opening of the town gates at night; they could take any route they pleased; they had first call on anybody's horses; and they could order all travellers ahead of them to clear out of the way, even if it meant going into the ditch. Langland points the difference in progress between the common man and the messenger:

> The merchant must need be let longer than the messenger;
> The messenger doth no more but with his mouth telleth
> His errand, and his letter sheweth, and is anon delivered. . . .
> Yet though they wenden on way as to Wynchester Fayre,
> The merchant with his merchandise may not go so swithe
> As the messenger may with so much ease.

But in all the varied company of those roads there is one type who is missing—the peasant or labourer. No worker, even when a free-man, was then allowed to travel; he must not, on pain of imprison-ment, go out of his own district without a permit, or passport, signed by the sheriff, which was not readily granted. This arose from the workers leaving a district where labour was plentiful, and going to another where it was scarce, and demanding (and receiving) higher wages than those generally ruling. Authority, as always, wanted to keep wages down, and decided that the easiest way of stopping this insolence of the workers was to forbid them all movement. It was felt, too, that by their wandering they were meeting their fellows from other districts (as we should say to-day, "getting together") and passing news and comparing notes; possibly hatching plots and risings. Hence the passport system, under which, according to Jusserand in his *English Wayfaring Life*, no man could leave his village without a letter issued by the sheriff or local justice, stating the cause of his going and the date by which he must return. To avoid forgery of those letters of travel, they had to bear a special seal showing the king's arms, the name of the county, and the name of the borough or hundred. Even when the worker wished to go on a religious pilgrimage, he could not go without one of those passports.

c*

The trials and perils of travel were little eased in the succeeding century. The roads were no better. In places where the Church did not attend to them, the responsibility was put upon the lord of the manor, who usually attended only to his own roads and left the highway to look after itself. And the lawlessness of earlier times persisted, and still made lonely wayfaring a matter of great personal hazard.

Contemporary accounts of journeys, and of proceedings before the magistrates, when certain towns were "presented" for not keeping their roads in repair, show that the general condition of the roads, even those on the outskirts of the capital, was scandalous. On one occasion, about the middle of the fifteenth century, when a Parliament was summoned, it had to be postponed because country members, owing to the foul and "jeopardous" state of the roads, could not reach London in time. Everybody agreed that such conditions were a scandal, and, in the English manner, everybody urged that somebody should do something about it. Farmers with farms near the highway helped themselves to its stones. Others dug soil from it. Dead cattle were left lying on it. If, in a tempest, trees fell and barred the way, it was nobody's business to remove them. Heavy rains invariably flooded the roads and turned them into quagmires full of pot-holes and pools in which a man might drown; and though causeways had been built at points where the road was near a river, many of these also had fallen to ruin. Often the condition of road or bridge compelled a traveller to go some miles out of his way to find a passage. If he were in haste he might set his horse to swim a river, knowing nothing of its depth; many travellers in this way lost their lives. Accidents were so common that they are mentioned only in passing, as something to be expected.

Ambush and robbery were another part of the natural incident of travel, and travellers usually set out with such an apprehension of disaster, from one cause or another, that before leaving they made their wills. In some parts of the country, bands of robbers rode about, waylaying travellers of all conditions, beating them as well as robbing them, and often taking even their clothes, and leaving them to perish of cold. The single highwayman, playing a lone hand, did not appear till the seventeenth century; in the fourteenth and fifteenth centuries robbery was always by bands, such as those mentioned in the Paston Letters. The road was lonely, and even though hedges and brushwood had been cut away from its border, there were often clumps of trees or dells or thickets, just off it, which made good hiding-places. Sometimes the road would be deliberately blocked by a felled tree, so that the awaited traveller would be compelled to leave the highway and cut across the common land, which would carry him past the hiding-place.

In the late fourteenth century, Chaucer, when he was Clerk of the Works to Richard, was twice robbed in one day on the road between London and Eltham Palace. He was travelling down with a sum of ten pounds for the settlement of some accounts when he was stopped by a gang of four young men, and robbed of money and horse. He returned to London to get another ten pounds, and on going down with it he was again robbed by the same band. He was held to account for the loss of the Royal twenty pounds, but after some time received Richard's "gracious" discharge.

The road was also used as the scene of the settlement of old scores. An affray in a town between two enemies would mean that one or both would be brought before the justices. But the countryside offered pools and ditches and caves, where bodies might lie for years undiscovered. A man would therefore wait until he heard that his enemy was going on a journey, and could learn the direction. He would then, with a few hired ruffians, set an ambush on the road, and that particular traveller would just disappear.

In the fifteenth century, as earlier, the cause of the neglect of the roads was the lack of any central authority or system. Their maintenance was still left almost wholly to local bodies and to casual private enterprise or philanthropy. This haphazard state of things is reflected in numerous wills of the period in which those with a thought for public welfare left sums of money for the upkeep or repair of specified roads, bridges, or causeways. William Langland shows the figure of Truth naming the various uses to which the wealthy may put their money for the general benefit, and includes the repair of roads:

> And wicked ways with their good amend,
> And bridges to-broke by the high-ways
> Amend in some manner wise . . .
> And I shall send you myself, St. Michael, mine angel,
> That no devil shall you dere, ne despair in your dying.

The presence on some bridges of little chapels, as at Bradford-on-Avon and Wakefield, is a reminder of the regard in which such benefactors were held. Anything done for the welfare of travellers was considered a service of piety, and the chapels were erected as memorials to the benefactors, and as shelters where tired travellers might rest and murmur a prayer for the repose of him whose bridge had eased their journey. A famous causeway, still to be seen outside

Chippenham, Wiltshire, was one of those pious gifts. A woman pedlar, Maud Heath, who, as a market-woman, had often to make her way along a flooded road, left at her death in 1474 a sum of money for the building of a causeway. Her memorial is not only the causeway itself. A sundial recording her gift was set up in 1698, and in 1830 a tall pillar, carrying a life-size statue of a woman pedlar, was set up and is known to all tourists in that district as Maud Heath's Pillar. Her bequests for the making of the causeway (eight pounds a year, some land and some houses) to-day produce enough to keep the whole length in perfect condition.

No signposts or milestones were then known, so that those travellers who were seeking their way in a strange country were compelled to hire a guide. For some centuries onward, the local guide who knew his country, and its byways and hidden tracks, was in constant service for cross-country journeys. Even as late as 1822 Cobbett had to hire a guide to put him on the way from Headley to Hindhead. Usually the guides were trustworthy, but sometimes they were incompetent, and contrived to get themselves and their traveller lost and benighted. Sometimes, too, we hear of rogues among them, in league with robbers, who would deliberately lead their traveller into an ambush. But few travellers going to a village or house off the highway, in a district new to them, could do without a guide.

The services of a guide were indeed imperative in the fording of rivers, or in taking short cuts at low tide across estuaries, such as those opening into Morecambe Bay; or in crossing the sands from the mainland to Holy Island. The crossing at low tide of the Wash, where King John lost his treasure—at that time it reached as far as Holbeach—saved a traveller many miles of roundabout travel, but none were so foolhardy as to attempt it without a guide. Even with a guide there were occasional fatalities in that fourteen-mile crossing. The crossing of Leven Sands, in the estuary of that Lancashire river, was so dangerous to those knowing nothing of the tides, or the difference between safe sands and quicksands, that in the fourteenth century the monks of Furness Abbey acted as voluntary guides, and on a little island in the estuary they built a chapel where, night and day, prayers were offered for the safety of those making the crossing. Another low-tide crossing, over Lancaster Sands, eleven miles in length, was supervised by the monks of Cartmel Priory, who also provided free guides; and yet another crossing, which was provided with guides, has a guide to this day.

And still, as the years went on, travel became no easier and no less hazardous. It was still linked, and the authorities seemed to wish it to be linked, with the word *travail*. Laws and orders came down from London concerning the maintenance of the roads, but they had little practical effect. By the late sixteenth century conditions were, if anything, worse. The suppression of the monasteries in 1539 had put an end to all the voluntary service which the Church had given, and there was as yet no organised and paid service to take its place. In winter the roads were sloughs and mires, or impassable with snow, and in summer the ruts were baked so hard that they would often overturn not only a horse but a waggon. The road between London and Norwich was an important road; yet at the end of the sixteenth century it was in places as unsound as any minor road of the fourteenth. The account written by Will Kemp, the morris-dancer, of his nine-days' dance from London to Norwich (he took four weeks over it) has several references to the tribulations of his journey caused by the state of the road. In each day's entry he speaks of "the foul way." Setting out one morning from Chelmsford:

> With hey and ho, through thick and thin,
> The hobby horse quite forgotten,
> I followed as I did begin,
> Although the way were rotten.

This foul way I could find no ease in, thick woods being on either side the lane: the lane likewise being full of deep holes, sometimes I skipt up to the waist. . . . It was the custom of honest country fellows my unknown friends, upon hearing of my Pipe (which might well be heard in a still morning or evening a mile) to get up and bear me company a little way. In this foul way two pretty plain youths watched me, and with their kindness somewhat hindered me. One a fine light fellow would be still before me, the other ever at my heels. At length coming to a broad plash of water and mud, which could not be avoided, I fetcht a rise, yet fell in over the ankles at the further end. My youth that follow'd me took his jump, and stuck fast in the midst.

The law ordained that once a year every common labourer of town and countryside was to give six days forced labour to helping in the repair of the roads in his district. Landowners and farmers were put under penalty to see that their men performed this duty. But the law got only perfunctory observance. Nobody likes working for nothing, so the men worked unwillingly, and managed so to spin out their labour that the six days might have been only two. Even then it was scamped. Further, the employers directed the labour mainly to repairing the roads leading to their own estates or farms, so that travellers received no benefit from the ordinance. The only time the roads of any district seem to have been in good repair was when a Royal Progress was expected. Then the whole town, to avoid Royal displeasure and heavy fines, turned to patching-up and gravelling.

Another abuse was that, with no special authority responsible for the road, those whose lands adjoined it began, yard by yard, to take portions of it to themselves, until its breadth diminished by more than half. William Harrison, in his *Description of Britain* (1577), after saying that he will speak nothing about this abuse, speaks thus:

> Of the daily encroaching of the covetous upon the highways I speak not. But this I know by experience, that whereas some streets within these five and twenty years have been in most places fifty foot broad according to the law, whereby the traveller might either escape the thief, or chift the mire, or pass by the loaden cart without danger of himself and his horse; now they are brought unto twelve, or twenty, or six and twenty at the most, which is another cause also whereby the ways be the worse, and many an honest man encumbered in his journey.

William Harrison was one of the earliest of that long line of explorers of England which has remained unbroken to this day. They travelled at that time, not for pleasure but for information; to penetrate the country up and down and across, to visit towns and harbours and rivers, and report what they had seen. They were not making official surveys such as that for the Domesday Book, or nosing into the private concerns of the great landowners; they wandered here and there at will, on horseback, noting this and that in the way of antiquities, contemporary buildings, large estates, mountains, roads, and forests. They showed none of the modern interest in the beauty of Nature or in landscape, and they say nothing of their personal adventures on the road. But they left us books of essential value; books which are used as a constant source of reference by all who wish to know something of the form and features of the England of that time.

The first was John Leland, whose *Itinerary*, embracing journeys made between 1533 and 1539, covers almost all England. The journeys were made with the approval of Henry, who had made him King's Antiquary and had given him authority to search where he would for records of things memorable or curious. William Harrison's work was something more than an account of an itinerary. It was a picture not only of the physical features of our island, but of its form of government, laws, flora and fauna, natural products, industries, and its social manners and customs. He was followed in 1586 by William Camden, with his *Britannia*, the most complete survey

then made of the British Isles; and from that time onward the
English road has never been empty of the curious and observant
traveller gathering facts and impressions, and setting them down in
volumes sometimes as brisk as a May morning and sometimes as leaden
as a January dawn.

The journeys of Leland and Harrison and Camden were much
more a trial of strength and spirit than those made by their successors
of the seventeenth and eighteenth centuries—strenuous as those later
journeys may seem to us of to-day. There were not only the foul
ways, and the many detours that had to be made, and the chance of
taking the wrong road, and being benighted. One had to be armed,
and not only against the professional robber, but against the sudden
amateur. All men, of course, travelled under arms, but some, as
William Harrison shows, went ferociously armed, as though to menace
the peaceful traveller or compel him, by mere display, to hand over:

> I might here speak of the excessive staves which divers that travel by
> the way do carry upon their shoulders, whereof some are twelve or thirteen
> feet long, beside the pike of twelve inches; but, as they are commonly
> suspected of honest men to be thieves and robbers, or at the leastwise
> scarce true men which bear them, so by reason of this and the like suspicious
> weapons the honest traveller is now forced to ride with a case of dags at
> his saddle-bow, or with some pretty short snapper, whereby he may deal
> with them further off in his own self-defence before he come within the
> danger of these weapons. Finally, no man travelleth by the way without
> his sword, or some such weapon, with us, except the minister, who com-
> monly weareth none at all, unless it be a dagger or hanger at his side.

Nor could one always trust the friendly fellow-traveller, nor always
be safe even in one's inn:

> Seldom also are they or any other wayfaring men robbed, without the
> consent of the chamberlain, tapster, or ostler where they bait and lie, who
> feeling at their alighting whether their capcases or budgets be of any weight
> or not, by taking them down from their saddles, or otherwise see their
> store in drawing of their purses, do by-and-by give intimation to some one
> or other attendant daily in the yard or house, or dwelling hard by, upon
> such matches, whether the prey be worth the following or no. If it be
> for their turn, then the gentleman peradventure is asked which way he
> travelleth, and whether it please him to have another guest to bear him
> company at supper, who rideth the same way in the morning that he doth.
> And thus if he admit him, or be glad of his acquaintance, the cheat is
> half wrought.

A traveller who missed his right road had no easy matter in finding it again from local directions. A phrase-book of 1593, for the use of foreigners, gives a realistic example of confused guidance:

> The way is very hard to be kept without a guide.
> Enquire of shepherds and shepherdesses whom you shall meet in travelling.
> Is the way dry and easy to keep?
> It is stony, and full of dangers by reason of theeves who lie in the woods.
> 'Tis a good country that has not one mile of naughty way.   Set me in my right way, I pray you.
> See you the gallows there on high?   Come not near it if you be wise; pass over the bridge, follow the pavement, hold the champain ground, leave the mountain, go along the vines, cross over the meadow, and you have always the highway before you.
> I doubt I shall miss my way.

Missing the way was a common adventure, even in the best circumstances, but Paul Hentzner, in his *Travels in England*, records an instance of being drawn out of his way by phantoms. The story recalls those desert phantoms of which Marco Polo tells, and later travellers have told. In the desert, it seems, it is considered highly dangerous for a man to get detached from his caravan. There are stories of men who have done this, and have heard their names called in voices they know, and, in following the sound, have met men resembling their fellow-travellers, and have gone some distance with them, into another part of the desert. They have then found that they are off the track and that the figures which lured them away have vanished into air. If it happens at night, it is said, they hear the noise of camel-bells to right or left of them. If they allow themselves to be drawn in that direction, away from their own company, they will be swallowed by the desert. Hentzner's little adventure was of that kind:

> *Canterbury:* we came to it on foot; this is the seat of the Archbishop, Primate of all England, a very ancient town, and, without doubt, of note in the time of the Romans. . . . Being tired with walking, we refreshed ourselves here with a mouthful of bread and some ale, and immediately mounted post-horses, and arrived about two or three o'clock in the morning at Dover.   In our way to it, which was rough and dangerous enough, the following accident happened to us: our guide or postillion, a youth, was before with two of our company, about the distance of a musket-shot; we, by not following quick enough, had lost sight of our friends; we came afterwards to where the road divided; on the right it was downhill and marshy, on the left was a small hill: whilst we stopped here in doubt, and consulted which of the roads we should take, we saw all on a sudden on

19 A Tudor Farmer's Wife returning from Market

20 A Packhorse leaving Tudor Aldgate

18 An Elizabethan Inn: "The Feathers," Ludlow

21 Some of Queen Elizabeth's Coaches

22 Queen Elizabeth on Progress through London in her State Litter

our right hand some horsemen, their stature, dress, and horses exactly resembling those of our friends; glad of having found them again, we determined to set on after them; but it happened, through God's mercy, that though we called to them, they did not answer us, but kept on down the marshy road at such a rate, that their horses' feet struck fire at every stretch, which made us, with reason, begin to suspect they were thieves, having had warning of such; or rather, that they were nocturnal spectres; who, as we were afterwards told, are frequently seen in those places: there were likewise a great many jack-a-lanterns, so that we were quite seized with horror and amazement. But fortunately for us, our guide soon after sounded his horn, and we, following the noise, turned down the left-hand road, and arrived safe to our companions; who, when we had asked them if they had not seen the horsemen who had gone by us, answered, not a soul.

More substantial impediments to the ordinary traveller were the Royal Progresses. They must have blocked for many miles the particular road the Royal personage was using, and no commoner, of course, could thrust past them. According to William Harrison, when Elizabeth travelled she carried all her possessions with her in 400 "carewares," using 2,400 horses, drawn from the adjoining districts. Another blocking of the roads, unhappily familiar to travellers of the fifteenth and sixteenth centuries, was caused by the Flight from London and other large towns. The evacuation of London by the scared, which we have seen during the last years, is nothing new; nor was the Great Plague of 1665 the first occasion of it. Plagues were too common in England, both before and after the Black Death of the fourteenth century. During a certain period they came every few years, and in the middle and later sixteenth century many writers produced pamphlets on the subject, some of them of a kind which, in to-day's jargon, might be calculated to cause despondency and alarm. In a lighter vein is William Bullein's *Dialogue Against the Pestilence*, written around a plague year of the middle of the century. With bright and homely chatter, he presents a citizen and his wife packing up and bolting from London, and, excepting the natural differences of period, it is just such a scene as we have all witnessed and heard from our windows, when the family car is drawn up next door:

"So now let's depart, a God's blessing, good wife."

"Give me my horse, Roger."

"Mistress, he is here ready at your hand, a good gelding. God bless him and sweet Saint Loye."

"Bring forth mine also, and let the servants forget nothing behind them,

specially the steel casket.   Let us ride fair and softly until we be out of
the town."

"How pleasant are these sweet fields, garnished with fair plants and
flowers.   The birds do sing sweetly and pitifully in the bushes; here are
pleasant woods.   Jesus, man, who would be in the city again?   Not I,
for an hundred pound. . . . I never was so far from London in all my life.
How far have we ridden already, sir, I pray you?"

"Wife, we have ridden ten miles this morning."

"What town is this, I pray you, sir?"

"This is Barnet, where Samuel your son was nursed; and yonder is
Richard Higmer's house; we will see him as we do return home again;
we will not tarry now, because every inn is pestered with Londoners and
carriers. . . . How like you this town, dame?"

"A pretty street; but methink the people go very plain; it is no city as I
do suppose by their manners.   What house is this at the town's end,
compassed with a moat?"

"Here dwelleth a friend of ours; this is called the Fold.   And here before
is Dancer's Hill and Rig Hill."

"What great smoke is in yonder wood?   God grant it be well."

"It is nothing but making of charcoal in that place."

About the middle of the sixteenth century, stage-waggons were
introduced for the general public.   These were not coaches, but long,
lumbering, springless, six-horsed vehicles, which would take days on a
journey from London to Winchester.   They were on the road up to
the end of the eighteenth century.   Private coaches also were introduced about the same time, but they were not taken into general
use.   According to a contemporary, the first coach seen in England
came from Holland.   It was presented by a Dutchman to Elizabeth,
who, until that time (1565) had not owned a coach.   Following the
royal example, a number of the wealthier men set up a coach, possibly
for its effect in increasing the owner's self-importance, and possibly
for its convenience in carrying the entire family and their baggage.
The baggage carried by the horse-traveller must have been considerable, since an early sixteenth-century pamphlet of advice to a
servant has a passage reminding the servant what his master will
need on a journey.   The list includes purse, dagger, cloak, nightcap,
shoe-horn, halter, saddle-cloth, horse-comb, sword, horn, gloves,
string, pen, ink, parchment, pen-knife, comb, needle and thread,
pieces of leather for repairing harness, as well as shirts, stockings, etc.

The coach therefore might have been a welcome innovation, but
generally it was frowned upon.   In the first year of the next century
an abortive Bill was brought in against it with the object of prevent-
ing its use by men, on the ground that it would make them indolent

and effeminate. Contemporary evidence shows, however, that a man had to be pretty tough to survive a long journey on the roads of that time in the kind of coach then available. Horseback continued generally to be the mode of travel, for women as well as men, since it not only allowed greater speed, but was actually less fatiguing. Elizabeth, on one occasion excused herself from some meeting with the plea of having been "knocked about in a coach driven too fast." Most of her Progresses were made by horse.

Travellers who did not own a horse of their own made their journeys by hiring horses from the posting-houses at a few pence per mile. These horses were used only for a short stage, about ten miles, when they were left at a given inn, and a new horse hired from that place. Often, of course, innkeepers lost their horses. The punishment for horse-stealing was death; the plea used to-day by "borrowers" of cars (joy ride) was not then heard of. But no penalty deterred the reckless, so individual innkeepers usually branded their horses with their own personal sign, which was known at all posting-houses along their particular road. Even so, they still occasionally lost a horse, sometimes when their own post-boy accompanied the hirer on a pillion-seat.

The case presented by Shakespeare in the *Merry Wives*, of the cheating of Mine Host of the Garter, was no isolated case. At that time, royalty, servants of royalty, and visiting princes could command horses from any inn or private stable for the pursuit of their journey, and settlement was made later from headquarters. When Bardolph announces that some Germans want three horses to meet their Duke, who is on his way to Court, the Host says they shall have his horses, but he will make them pay. "I'll sauce them: they have had my house a week at command; I have turned away my other guests: they must come off; I'll sauce them." A little later, Bardolph returns without the horses:

Bard: Out, alas, sir. Cozenage, mere cozenage.

Host: Where be my horses? Speak well of them, varletto.

Bard: Run away with the cozeners; for so soon as I came beyond Eton, they threw me off from behind one of them in a slough of mire; and set spurs and away, like three German devils, three Doctor Faustuses.

Host: They are gone but to meet the Duke, villain. Do not say they be fled: Germans are honest men.

Enter Sir Hugh Evans.

Evans: Where is mine host?

Host: What is the matter, sir?

Evans: Have a care of your entertainments: there is a friend of mine

D

come to town, tells me there is three cozen-germans that has cozened all the hosts of Reading, of Maidenhead, of Colebrook, of horses and money. I tell you for goodwill, look you: you are wise and full of gibes and vlouting-stogs, and 'tis not convenient you should be cozened. Fare you well. [*Exit.*

Enter Dr. Caius.

Caius: Vere is mine host de Jartiere?

Host: Here, Master doctor, in perplexity and doubtful dilemma.

Caius: I cannot tell vat is dat; but it is tell-a me dat you make grand preparation for a duke de Jarmany: by my trot, dere is no duke de court is know to come. I tell you for good vill: adieu. [*Exit.*

Host: Hue and cry, villain! Go. Assist me, knight; I am undone. Fly, run, hue and cry, villain! I am undone!

Urgent riders often changed their horses at less than ten-mile intervals, and made record rides. A notable ride was that of Sir Robert Carey. In the thirteenth century, the herald of the King of Scotland, for a journey from London to Scotland, was allowed forty days. In the fourteenth century, a fugitive rode from Gloucester to Scotland in seven days, which was only just a little better than the general rate of travel for those days. The first real high-speed achievement was that of Carey. Elizabeth was dying. Carey, as hungry as all courtiers of those days were for jobs and places and many of them, waited at Greenwich for her death. When it was a fact, he went to London, and from there set out for Edinburgh ahead of all the other place-hunters, in the hope of being the first to salute the new king.

He left London at ten o'clock on a Thursday morning. By nightfall he had reached Doncaster. On Friday night he got to his own house at Witherington. By noon of Saturday he got to the Border. But during Saturday's journey his horse fell and threw him and kicked him on the head, and with the loss of blood he became so faint that he had to moderate his pace. Had he kept his customary pace, he would have been with the king that afternoon. But, even as it was, he pressed on at the best pace he could make, reached Edinburgh just as the king was going to bed, and got the job he had gone after—one of the Lords of the Bedchamber. On wretched and broken roads, he made the journey in about sixty hours of riding-time—a record that stood until the third quarter of the seventeenth century, when William Nevison, the highwayman, took it with his ride from Rochester to York in one day: 220 miles in sixteen hours. But so slow, in the ordinary way, was the passage of news, that in parts of Devon and Cornwall her death was not heard of till the Court was out of mourning.

While the roads of the sixteenth century were almost as bad as in the Middle Ages, the inns of that time showed great improvement. The town tavern may have been somewhat squalid in its appointments, and some of the village ale-houses may have been like that of John Skelton's Elinor Rummyng; but the general run of the town inns "for the receipt of travellers" were notable for their fine furniture, their cleanliness, and their large hospitality. "Our inns," says Harrison, "are also very well furnished with napery; bedding and tapestry especially with napery; for beside the linen used at the tables, which is commonly washed daily, is such and so much as belongeth unto the estate and calling of the guest. Each comer is sure to lie in clean sheets, wherein no man has been lodged since they came from the laundress." He speaks also of the "furniture of bedding, beauty of rooms, service at the table, costliness of plate, strength of drink, variety of wines," and of the gorgeousness of the signs, some of them costing thirty or forty pounds.

This general picture of the inn is an indication of the throbbing business that was coming to the roads, and the increase of travel. Inns of noble appointment were opened not only in towns but at points along the road. The derelict monastic hostels were renovated and fitted as public inns and posting-houses, with all comforts for travellers. Decayed mansions were taken over and turned to public use, and innkeepers competed with each other in the furnishing of their rooms and in the service they gave, and in their material welcome to their guests, such as a glass of canary or sherris, and little snacks on arriving. Carpets replaced rushes; forks—though at first considered what we now call sissy—were used instead of fingers; and at dinner or supper the company no longer dipped into a common dish. Music at meals, if only the town waits or the local ballad-singer, was provided, an innovation not always appreciated even in those lusty days, and one that we of to-day have no cause to bless.

It was a time of stir and change and new ideas in many things; and among the things that were then established as part of the English tradition was the spirit of the good English inn. From then onward, the cheerful, comely, hospitable inn has been a permanent and delightful feature of the English road and the social scene, and, in spirit and substance, a piquant garnish to travel.

CHAPTER TWO
Stuart Travellers

THROUGHOUT THE seventeenth century the traffic of the roads thickened and thickened. There was not only the traffic of trade and private business. Men were more and more travelling, not for the sake of travelling, as we of to-day do, but in a spirit of inquiry, observing and noting, in the way of Leland and Camden. They could not reconcile themselves to travelling without an object; and indeed, travelling, even as late as that century, could have been no matter of mere pleasure. Also, to some extent an object was necessary: travellers on the road were sometimes asked to give an account of themselves, where they were going, and why.

Those "curious" travellers were not without their critics. In later times English travel became almost an industry; people were urged to travel and to see their own country. But there was always, especially among the divines, a certain sourness to new-fangled ways, and in 1617 the Rev. Joseph Hall let out against travellers, and wanted to know why they couldn't improve their minds in their own chairs:

> There are two occasions wherein travel may pass—matter of traffic and matter of state. It is the travel of curiosity wherewith my quarrel shall be maintained, the inconvenience whereof my own senses have so sufficiently witnessed, that if the wise parents of our gentry could have borrowed my eyes for the time they would ever learn to keep their sons at home. I have known some that have travelled no further than their own closet, which could both teach and correct the greatest traveller after all his tedious and costly pererrations. Let an Italian or French passenger walk through this our island, what can his table-books carry home in comparison of the learned *Britaine* of our Camden or the accurate tables of Speed? With these helps let us travel by our own fireside. A good book is at once the best companion and guide, and way and end of our journey. Necessity drove our forefathers out of doors, which else in those misty times had seen no light; we may with more ease and no less profit sit still.

Hackney-coaches, for use in and about London, were introduced during the early years of Charles I. Stage-coaches did not appear till about the middle of the century. They had not appeared in Fynes Moryson's time, since he speaks only of coaches for private hire and of the carrier's waggon. Those private coaches could not be hired on the road or in country towns, only in London:

23 An Elizabethan Coach arriving at Montacute, Somerset
A reconstruction by Joseph Nash

24 A contemporary engraving of a Seventeenth-Century Coach

25 A Party outside an Inn, 1699

26 Shoeing a Horse, 1699

(Both from engravings by Hohburg)

Coaches are not to be hired anywhere but only at London; and howsoever England is for the most part plain, or consisting of pleasant hills, yet the ways far from London are so dirty as hired coachmen do not ordinarily take any long journeys, but only for one or two days any way from London, the ways so far being sandy and very fair and continually kept so by labour of hands. . . . Sixty or seventy years ago coaches were very rare in England, but at this day pride is so far increased, as there be few gentlemen of any account who have not their coaches, so as the streets of London are almost stopped up with them. Yea, they who only respect comeliness and profit, and are thought free from pride, yet have coaches; because they find the keeping thereof more commodious and profitable than of horses, since two or three coach-horses will draw four or five persons, besides the commodity of carrying many necessaries in a coach. For the most part Englishmen, especially in long journeys, use to ride upon their own horses. . . . Likewise, carriers let horses from city to city, with caution that the passenger must lodge in their inn, that they may look to the feeding of their horses. . . . Lastly, these carriers have long covered waggons, in which they carry passengers from city to city: but this kind of journeying is so tedious, by reason that they must take waggon very early, and come very late to their inns, as none but women and people of inferior condition or strangers use to travel in this sort.

The same authority tells us that the majority of travellers made no pause for dinner, which was then about two o'clock. They rode continuously, from breakfast to supper-time, and got early to their night's inn so that the horses should have full rest. At the inn they could take their supper either at the "ordinary" or in a private room. If they took it with the host or at the common table, the cost was usually sixpence; but men of "condition" seldom condescended to this. They had a table set in the "Dolphin" or the "Half Moon" or the "Rose," and ordered what they would, and were free to visit the kitchen and see that their dishes were dressed to their own taste.

They had a rather wider choice than the traveller of to-day, and as they moved from county to county, so their diet varied every few days. They did not have to dine in Somerset and Northumberland and Suffolk and Hampshire on our eternal country-hotel dinner of tomato soup, fried plaice, roast lamb, roast chicken, and stewed prunes. Game was not then the dish of the few; it was everyman's meat; and the host could usually furnish one or two selections from woodcock, duck, snipe, plover, partridge, pigeon, hare, boar, peacock, badger, kid, and venison. For fish, he could furnish lampreys, elvets, sturgeon, pike, chub, and carp; and among his fruits were quinces, medlars, citrons, pearmains, mulberries, apricots, green figs, and local nuts.

D*

And he could always offer some regional dish peculiar to his own county, and made nowhere else. There were the Cambridge brawn, the Kentish huffkin, the Northumberland singing-hinnie, the Norfolk cygnet, the Somerset laver, the Devonshire junket, the Grantham whetstone, the Banbury cheese, the Cornish pasty; things that the traveller would not find in his own corner of England. Indeed, when he was a hundred miles from his home, he was almost in a new country, with different customs, different clothes, and different forms of speech, some of which were incomprehensible to him. Sussex and Yorkshire, Cornwall and Norfolk, were separated in more matters than distance, and at that time a journey from one to the other had more rewards and surprises than it offers to-day.

An interesting account of the rewards and surprises of a tour of discovery, made some ten years before the Civil War, is given in *A Survey of Twenty-six Counties Observed in a Seven Weeks Journey* by a Captain, a Lieutenant, and an Ancient [Ensign]. This existed only as a manuscript in the British Museum until 1904, when it was published in an edition of 350 copies, with an Introduction by A. G. Wickham Legg. The three soldiers were the new sort of traveller, out to remark the remarkable, wherever they might find it, whether it were a mansion, a monument, a relic, an abominable road, or the host of their inn. They seem to have found some very dangerous roads and some very agreeable hosts.

At Lincoln they did not see their host on their arrival: he had "bouz'd it so" that he had gone to bed early; but in the morning they found him a right good fellow. At Newark they stayed at the Saracen's Head, where the host was "as jovial as twenty good fellows: his name, agreeing with his mirth, was Twentyman." They describe him as looking like a beef-eating Guard-boy and a very good intelligencer. When he learned the object of their journey, he performed the duty commonly performed by innkeepers to travellers at that time: he took them out and showed them the sights of the town, and introduced them here and there. At supper he kept them so entertained with "mirth, merry tales, and true jests" that, tired as they were, they had no thought of bed.

At their inn at York they found a "loving, gentle widow," who behaved more like a mother than the hostess of an inn. When she heard of their arrival, in bad weather, wet and weary, she came down and received them with a glass of sherry and a dish of fresh salmon, and they noted a peculiarity of northern speech in her words of welcome—"Marry, God thank ye for making my house your harbour."

At Robin Hood's Well it was the custom for travellers to be stopped

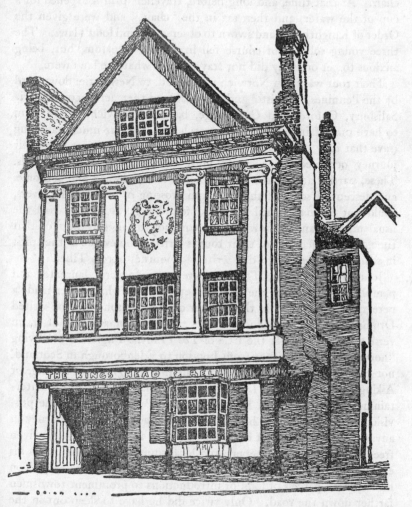

The "King's Head and Bell" at Abingdon: an English Inn of the
Seventeenth Century

and put through one of those facetious ceremonies of different kinds held at many places on the road.   Robin Hood's Well was, and is, a natural spring coming from a rock formation in the form of a rough chair.   At that time, and long before, travellers paid fourpence for a cup of the water, and then sat in the "chair," and were given the Order of Knighthood, and sworn to observe Robin Hood's laws.   The three young soldiers of course fell in with the custom, but, being anxious to get on, they did not stay to learn what the laws were.

Their tour was from Norwich northward, to Newcastle; downward by the Pennines, to Bristol and the west; and then across country, via Salisbury, Oxford, and Cambridge, back to Norwich.   They seem to have made fairly good progress each day, without much dawdling (save that they did no travelling on Sundays), and the fact that their journey occupied seven weeks must be attributed to the roads. These, particularly in the north, they found awkward and toilsome, and descent of some of the hills, and crossing of some of the rivers, could not be made until they had found a guide.   They had the usual mishaps and narrow escapes common to all travellers of that time, and the account of their tour is written somewhat in the spirit in which travellers of to-day write of a journey across Tibet.

John Taylor, sailor, Thames waterman, doggerel laureate, and pamphleteer, known as the Water Poet, had somewhat earlier made a peregrination on foot, in the manner of Ben Jonson when he visited Drummond of Hawthornden.   He published an account of it, in verse and prose, under the title of *The Pennyles Pilgrimage*, showing "how he travailed on foot from London to Edenborough in Scotland, not carrying any Money to or fro, neither Begging, Borrowing, or Asking Meate, drinke or Lodging; With his Description of his Entertainment in all places of his journey. . . . "   He carried some provisions with him, but as he had apparently advertised his journey in advance, and the style of it, he was received as a curiosity, and given free hospitality by innkeepers and local squires.   In some places his entertainment was lavish, and he was almost everywhere helped on his way with parcels of food or introductions to prominent townsmen farther down the road.   Only twice did he have to sleep out in the fields, and only once did he go without food for as long as twenty hours.

Setting out from Aldersgate at sunset, he got only as far as Islington before dark.   There he was given a carousal and a lodging and a morning send-off.   The second night was spent at St. Albans.   On the road next morning, a horseman who recognised him and knew of his journey, offered him money.   The conditions under which he had

27 A Seventeenth-Century Stage-Wagon climbing a hilly road

Detail from a contemporary engraving

28 A Rest by the Roadside in the Seventeenth Century, showing
a contemporary Litter

30 "John Cottington, *alias* Mull Sack,

29 "Captain Hind robbing Colonel Harrison

set out forbade his accepting this, but he said he would gladly drink its value. When he reached Hockcliffe, he found that the horseman had paid for, and left for him, a jug of ale. That night he reached Stony Stratford, and received free accommodation at the local inn. On the road to Daventry, another horseman told him he would leave refreshment for him in the town, but at Daventry the crowd that came out to see him was so thick that, while he was being greeted, certain low fellows drank off the ale that had been left for him. The hostess of the inn, whom he describes without much chivalry, saw this, but did not interfere, and would not replenish the jug. Nor did she offer him food or a night's rest, which he seemed to expect as a right. At Coventry, Philemon Holland entertained him for two days, and at Lichfield too he received entertainment. But between Lichfield and Newcastle-under-Lyne he had a rough passage. Nobody treated him; nobody offered him food or shelter:

> That Wednesday I a weary way did pass,
> Rain, wind, stones, dirt, and dabbling dewy grass,
> With here and there a pelting scattered village,
> Which yielded me no charity or pillage:
> For all the day, nor yet the night that followed,
> One drop of drink I'm sure my gullet swallowed.
> At night I came to a stony town called Stone,
> Where I knew none, nor was I known of none:
> I therefore through the streets held on my pace,
> Some two miles farther to some resting-place. . . .

He had to camp out in a hayfield, under an improvised tent of boughs and twigs, without food or drink, in an all-night downpour. Macclesfield was a compensation: there he had four days' hospitality; and a letter of introduction to Manchester brought him two nights and a day of hospitality. On the liquor side, the hospitality was unceasing and almost overwhelmed him. He was put up at the Eagle and Child inn, whose hostess had his linen washed, and sent him on his way with a store of bacon. His charges were borne by the man to whom he carried the letter of introduction, who also lent him a guide to see him through the rest of Lancashire. At Preston, the leading innkeeper gave him three days' entertainment, and the Mayor came to visit him, and, on his leaving, accompanied him some miles out of the town and introduced him to the under-sheriff of the county. This new patron took him to Lancaster, where the jailer, who also kept an inn, entertained him for two days, and sent him on with a guide through Westmorland to Sedbergh.

And so the tale goes on. All through his account he advertises and belauds those who fed him and sped him, and is notably laudatory

in his remarks on Scotland and the Scotch. The return journey was
made by horse, accompanied by a Scot who was travelling to London,
and who paid all his expenses. He gives a picture of Scottish
hospitality at an inn at Cockburnspath, which, despite all one has
heard (if not always experienced) of that country's liberality, seems
incredible:

> So that night he brought me to a place called Cockburnspath, where we
> lodged at an inn the like of which, I dare say, is not in any of his Majesty's
> dominions. And for to show my thankfulness to Master William Arnot
> and his wife, the owners thereof, I must explain their bountiful entertain-
> ment of guests, which is this. Suppose ten, fifteen, or twenty men and
> horses come to lodge at their house, the men shall have flesh, tame and
> wild fowl, fish, with all variety of good cheer, good lodging, and welcome;
> and the horses shall want neither hay nor provender, and at the morning
> at their departure the reckoning is just nothing. This is the worthy
> gentleman's use, his chief delight being only to give strangers entertain-
> ment gratis.

On other tours he was not so fortunate, and complains in rather
harsh terms of having to sleep with shepherds or, as the guest of a
humble cottager, on the floor. He was specially harsh about an
occasion when the servants of a great house would not accord him the
benighted traveller's right of sleeping in their quarters. But he
knew what belonged to His Majesty's Water Poet, and anyway he
was a commander of harsh terms, as in his pamphlet of invective
against the introduction of hackney-coaches, which had ruined his
business and that of hundreds of other watermen.

Another of his pamphlets was an alphabetical Guide to country
carriers, giving the towns to which they went from London, the inns
of London from which they set out, and their day of arrival and
departure: "whereby all sorts of people may find direction how to
receive or send goods or letters unto such places as their occasions
may require." The Guide also gave similar information about the
ships, hoys, barques, barges, and wherries, and the particular Thames
quay at which vessels for coastal and estuary towns could be found.
The carrier's cart was used not only for the transport of goods, but
it was, as shown above, a postal service. Letters for distant places
were passed from carrier to carrier, as Taylor shows in his preface:

> If a carrier of York hath a letter or goods to deliver at any town in his
> way thither, he serves the turn well enough; and there are carriers and
> messengers from York to carry such goods and letters as are to be passed
> any ways north, broad and wide as far or farther than Berwick. So he
> that sends to Lancaster may from thence have what he sends conveyed to

Kendal or Cockermouth; and what a man sends to Hereford may from thence be passed to St. Davids in Wales. The Worcester carriers can convey anything as far as Caermarthen; and those that go to Chester may send to Carnarvon. The carriers or posts that go to Exeter may send daily to Plymouth or to the Mount in Cornwall . . . so likewise all the towns and places are served which are betwixt London and Lincoln, or Boston, Yarmouth, Oxford, Cambridge, Walsingham, or any place of the King's dominions, with safe and true carriage.

His Guide does not waste words; he is almost as concise as Bradshaw:

The Carriers of Barnstaple in Devonshire do lodge at the Star in Bread Street. They come on Fridays and return on Saturdays or Mondays.

The Carriers of Cambridge do lodge at the Bell in Coleman Street. They come every Thursday.

The Carriers of Halifax in Yorkshire do lodge at the Greyhound in Smithfield. They do come but once every month.

The water-transport notes are equally terse:

The Reading boat is to be had at Queenhithe weekly.

A Hoy doth come from Colchester in Essex to Smart's Key near Billingsgate.

He that will send to Ipswich in Suffolk, or Lynn in Norfolk; let him go to Dice Key, and there his turn may be served.

The carrier of those days was a familiar and important figure of the road, second only to the official messenger. He knew his road as townsmen knew their own street, and everybody on the road knew him. He enjoyed the full confidence of those who used his services: anything could be entrusted to him in the knowledge that (barring highwaymen) it would be safely delivered. He carried, as well as letters, oral messages, love-tokens, and news. He must have been subject to many temptations, yet generally he is presented as a character of complete honesty and integrity, proud of his calling and jealous of his good name. He was on the road in all weathers, in wind and flood and snowstorm, trudging alongside his team up hill and down, covering about the same number of miles each day, and coming each night to the inn appointed for that night. John Earle, in his *Microcosmography*, has a sketch of the type:

A carrier . . . is like the vault in Gloucester church that conveys whispers at a distance, for he takes the sound out of your mouth at York and makes it be heard as far as London. . . . He is a great afflicter of the highways, and beats them out of measure, which injury is sometimes revenged by the purse-taker, and then the voyage miscarries. No man domineers more in his inn, nor calls his host unreverently with more presumption, and this arrogance proceeds out of the strength of his horses. He forgets not his load where he takes his ease, for he is drunk commonly before he goes to bed.

Milton, too, sketched the type in his two pieces on the death of Hobson, the Cambridge carrier, who died, it seems, of boredom when he was forbidden, because of the Plague, to make his usual journeys:

> Here lieth one who did most truly prove
> That he could never die while he could move;
> So hung his destiny, never to rot
> While he might still jog on and keep his trot. . . .
> Rest, that gives all men life, gave him his death,
> And too much breathing put him out of breath. . . .

The carrier was brother to the Jolly Waggoner, who drove the stage-waggons. Both were cheerful, honest fellows, ruddy with sun and wind and ale; the waggoner, perhaps, the more cheerful, since he had his company of passengers to talk to, while the carrier had to make his journey alone. The waggoner, like the carrier, did not drive with reins from a driving-seat. He had to walk most of his journey at the head of the leading horse, or ride an extra horse alongside the team. Driving from the waggon was forbidden, because of the danger of his falling asleep.

These stage-waggons were used only by the poorer people. Their rate of travel at that time was about two miles an hour. They usually managed to do about twenty miles a day, and the charge on most roads was a halfpenny a mile. The waggon-party, on setting out, would choose among themselves a leader or fugleman, who would deal with the waggoner on all matters concerning his passengers. The length of the day's journey and the night's halting-place were decided by general vote, and the waggoner halted, or pushed on another stage, according to their wishes. The waggons of those days had no seats. The passengers sat on the floor among straw or on any bales of soft goods the waggon might be carrying. At their inns—or rather their hedge ale-houses, since they could hardly rise to inns—they slept in the barn or hay-loft or other outhouse; or they might sleep in the waggon itself, or, in summer, in the open. Supper was served for the party at a lump sum, arranged by the fugleman, to which all contributed.

Samuel Sorbière, a Frenchman who visited England in 1663, and wrote an account of his travels, described how he rode from Dover to London in the stage-waggon, and gave a rapid sketch of the waggoner. He seems to have thought that the stage-waggon was a degree above, instead of below, the stage-coach.

That I might not take post, or be obliged to make use of the stage-coach, I went from Dover to London in a waggon, it was drawn by six horses one before another, and drove by a waggoner, who walked by the side of it: he was clothed in black, and appointed in all things like another St. George; he had a brave mounteero on his head, and was a merry fellow, fancy'd he made a figure, and seemed mightily pleased with himself. It's necessary I should observe to you, for the better understanding of what I shall say concerning the humour of the nation, and the appearance the people make in city and country, that you will meet with no faces there that move pity, nor no habit that denotes misery. . . .

He goes on to say that while England has many poor people their poverty is not so great as in other countries, and is due to idleness. When once the poor people have obtained the necessaries of life, their natural laziness and a certain pride make them disinclined to chase after any more. He had not a very high opinion of his travelling companions:

I shall not enter upon a detail of the entertainment we met with upon the road, because I understood it not; but I learnt from a Zeelander, with whom I spoke Flemish, that the English made large reckonings, that the people were of a railing and back-biting temper. . . . They are very civil to one another, and use much circumspection in their conversation. But he is unhappy that cannot keep pace with them in their language, for they are not wanting in making their advantage of those who do not understand it. . . . My fellow travellers not only declined in their inns to take care as they ought of a stranger, who could not tell how to make the people understand him, but I was as little regarded as if I had been a bale of goods; nay, there were attempts made to incommode me.

The precise time when stage-coaches were first put on the roads is a matter of conjecture. It seems to have been some time between 1650 and 1660, though just before the first date the gadabout John Taylor issued a pamphlet describing a journey by the weekly South-ampton coach that went from Holborn. One of the earliest coaches ran to Chester (six days). Others, put on the road in succeeding years, went to Exeter (eight days), York (eight days), Bath (three days), and Oxford (two days)—though one enterprising innkeeper set up, for the reckless, a coach that did London–Oxford in one day. Taylor's coach stopped two nights on the road, and reached Southampton only during the third day:

We took our coach, two coachmen and four horses,
And merrily from London made our courses.
We wheeled the top of th' heavy hill called Holborne
(Up which hath been full many a sinful soul borne)

E

And so along we jolted past St. Gileses,
Which place from Brainford [Brentford] six or near seven miles is.
To Stanes that night at five o'clock we coasted,
Where (at the Bush) we had baked, boiled and roasted.
Bright Sol's illustrious rays the day adorning,
We past Bagshot and Baw-waw Friday morning.
That night we lodged at the White Hart at Alton,
And had good meat—a table with a salt on. . . .

Those early coaches ran during the summer months only; they
were taken off each November and did not reappear until the
spring. But by the last quarter of the century, a number of them
were running right through the year, though on the long journeys,
where the summer time was six days, the winter time was eight; and
where it was four days, it became six. The coaches themselves were
cumbrous things, and the stresses and strains they had to endure
on broken or rutted roads, with no effective springs, brought frequent
breakdowns. The sufferings of the coaches were shared by the
passengers. Often, during the journey, they became ill from the
swaying and jolting, and at the end of it many of them had to lay up
for a day or so. Possibly the author of a pamphlet calling for the
suppression of stage-coaches, John Cresset, was inspired to make his
attack after one or two tentative journeys. He has nothing good to
say of them:

What advantage is it to men's health to be called out of their beds
into their coaches an hour before day in the morning, to be hurried in
them from place to place till one, two, or three hours within night, inso-
much that sitting all day in the summer-time stifled with heat and choked
with dust, or in the winter-time starving or freezing with cold, or choked
with filthy fogs? They are often brought to their inns by torchlight, when
it is too late to sit up to get a supper, and next morning they are forced
into the coach so early that they can get no breakfast. . . . Is it for a
man's health to travel with tired jades, to be laid fast in foul ways, and
forced to wade up to the knees in mire; afterwards sit in the cold till
teams of horses can be sent to pull the coach out? . . . Is it for a man's
pleasure, or advantageous to their healths and business to travel with a
mixt company that he knows not how to converse with; to be affronted
by the rudeness of a surly, dogged, cursing, ill-natured coachman; necessi-
tated to lodge or bait at the worst inns on the road, where there is no
accommodation fit for gentlemen; and this merely because the owners of
the inns and the coachmen are agreed together to cheat the guests?

Travelling by stage-coach may have been all that Cresset says
against it, but travelling generally, by any means, was beginning to
be recognised, if not as a pleasure, at least as conferring the benefit

of recreation. Henry Peachum, author of *The Compleat Gentleman* and other works, in another of his pamphlets, goes clean against Joseph Hall, and recommends it as good both for the body and the mind. So good, indeed, that he can hardly find enough exclamation notes:

> But the truth is, the most pleasing of all is riding with a good horse and a good companion, in the spring or summer season, into the country, when the blossoms are on the trees and flowers in the fields; or when corn and fruit are ripe in autumn. What sweet and goodly prospects shall you have on both sides of you upon the way! delicate green fields! low meadows! diversity of crystal streams! woody hills! parks with deer! hedgerows! orchards! fruit trees! churches! villages! the houses of gentlemen and husbandmen! several habits and faces! variety of country labours and exercises! And if you happen, as it often falleth out, to converse with countrymen of the place, you shall find them, for the most part, understanding enough to give you satisfaction: and sometimes country maids and market wenches will give as unhappy answers as they be asked knavish and uncivil questions. Others there be, who, out of their rustical simplicity, will afford you matter of mirth. . . .

He seems to find nothing in bad roads or the mischances of travel so often mentioned by other writers. And he says nothing of an ever-present danger of the seventeenth-century road—the highwayman. The highwayman of that time was most prominent in years of peace. When wars were on, he could usually find subsistence by offering his sword. When there was no war, he found that the abilities of courage and hardihood that served him in the field were of little value in earning a living in town or country. So he took to the road, and in most cases came to what was called a bad end, though, according to Captain Johnson and other biographers of the tobymen, he always died penitent.

One of the brotherhood, who came to repentance after capture and condemnation, escaped the bad end. He was reprieved on a petition to Charles I, and, in gratitude, he wrote in the King's Bench prison a full confession of his misdeeds: *A Recantation of an Ill-Ledde Life*. On his title-page he describes himself, with some assurance: John Clavel, *Gent*. The pamphlet is in doggerel verse, and it not only expresses his humble, and rather overdone, repentance: it purports to give away all the secrets of highwaymen and their tricks in effecting a hold-up and getting away; what we now call the Inside Dope. Like most things of the kind, it discloses little that was not then generally known by all travellers except the very simple. He shows us the ambush and the preparations for stopping the approaching travellers:

So being come together, there you lie
In some odd corner, whence you may descry
Such booties as shall pass, and then says he
That is the oldest thief—be ruled by me.
And mark what I shall say. Thus must you place
Your masks and chin-clothes; thus then you your face
May soon disguise, and what is he can swear
Directly and precisely who we were?
And that your words may yield a differing tone,
Put in your mouths each one a pebble stone.
Now must we choose a watch-word somewhat common
As (*what's a clock*) for fear lest we should summon
Their thoughts into suspicion; then be sure,
The word once named, each man to deal secure;
We that are strongest at the gripe will seize;
Then be assured for to observe me these—
With your left hand to catch the bridle fast,
And let the right upon the sword be cast.
The one prevents escaping, t'other then
Quells their resistance. Let our weaker men
That are not thus employed, cry boldly Stand,
And with their swords and pistols them command.

He warns his readers against travelling on Sundays. "God in the way oft meets with him"—in the form of a highwayman. The high-wayman often worked on Sundays because then the roads were quiet, and further, he knew that any man so profane as to travel on Sunday must have very urgent business, and therefore will have money on him for the pursuit of that business. And if any man, travelling on a Sunday, did fall a victim, he had no redress in law. A traveller robbed on the highway during the week could claim against the borough or hundred in which the robbery happened. He could cause the local people to raise hue and cry, and if the robber were not taken, the borough or hundred had to make good to him the amount he had lost. Sometimes, according to Clavel, travellers surrendered their money to a single robber without a struggle, and then reported that they were set upon by three or four men for whom they were no match; and often doubled the sum they had lost. But if they were robbed on a Sunday, no claim was allowed.

He further warns the traveller to avoid, if possible, the high road, and travel on minor roads. Highwaymen did not bother with byways. There might now and then be a pretty haul on a byway, but one might have to wait days for the chance of it, while the highway brought a constant flow from whom they could choose. He also warns the traveller, setting out on a journey, not to follow the usual custom of calling his friends together and giving a little feast at which they will drink success and a safe return; he should tell nobody of his intended journey, since highwaymen have many sources of information. He should avoid riding in a group. The highwaymen can surround a group, and deal with them at pleasure; but if, say, four friends are sharing a journey, they should ride in single file, a hundred yards between each of them. That makes it awkward for the highwaymen, since, while they are dealing with the leading man, the man at the rear may get away and raise the alarm.

He also advises travelling at night. Highwaymen, apparently, assumed that nobody travelled at night, and they did not themselves care for being out at night. They might have to explain at their inns or lodgings why they came home at two or three o'clock in the morning, and where they had been. Again, the dark gave them no chance of seeing what the situation was; whether they were safe from interruption; how many the travellers were; or, if a single traveller, whether he had the appearance of carrying valuables, or whether he carried pistols.

He has a final word on how to catch a highwayman after a robbery. It is useless to send hue and cry up and down the road on which you were robbed. If you were robbed, say, at Colnbrook, it is waste of the constables' time to search the Bath road. Your highwayman will cut at once down a side road, and must be looked for on the Uxbridge road or the Staines road. If you are robbed at Hampstead, you must get the officers of the peace to search the taverns of Southwark and Lambeth; if at Kensington, then search at Aldgate.

He mentions one or two other ways of dealing with your highwayman, or avoiding him, but he does not mention George Fox's way. George Fox, the Quaker, was constantly on the road, carrying the truth and the light to any part of England to which he was moved to go; and he was constantly being man-handled and battered by angry priests and furious townsmen, and was in and out of prison. But he was never assaulted by highwaymen. He had a short way with them, as his one encounter shows:

> Once as I was going with Colonel Osburne to his house, there lay a company of rude fellows by the wayside, hid under the hedges and in bushes. Spying them, I asked him what they were. "Oh," said he, "they are thieves." Robert Widders, being moved to go and speak to a priest, was left behind, intending to come after. So I said to Colonel Osburne, "I will stay here in this valley, and do thou go look after Robert Widders"; but he was unwilling to go, being afraid to leave me there alone, because of those fellows, till I told him I feared them not. Then I called to them, asking them what they lay lurking there for, and I bid them

E*

come up to me; but they were loth to come. I charged them to come up
to me, or else it might be worse with them. Then they came trembling,
for the dread of the Lord had struck them. I admonished them to be
honest, and directed them to the light of Christ in their hearts, that by it
they might see what an evil it was to follow after theft and robbery; and
the power of the Lord came over them.

John Evelyn had not the hypnotic power of George Fox, and in his
encounter on a midsummer day with two footpads, he came off
badly. He was attacked on the road near Bromley. They struck
at his horse, snatched the reins from his hands, pulled him off, took
his sword, and dragged him into a thicket about a quarter-mile from
the road, where they went through his baggage and pockets. Then
they bound his hands, took off his riding boots, and bound his feet,
and fixed him against an oak tree, "with most bloudy threats to cutt
my throat if I offered to crie out or make any noise." He told them
that if they had not surprised him they would not have had so easy
a prize, and that it would teach him never to ride near a hedge;
"had I ben in the mid-way they durst not have adventured on me."
They did not take his horse: it was too well marked. They tied it
to a tree, so that it could graze, and went off.

For two hours he had to endure sun and ants and flies, until, after
continued struggling, he was able to turn his hands, which had been
tied back to back, and to slip one thumb free, and at last to get the
hand free. When he was fully unbound, he got his horse and rode
to the nearest justice to raise hue and cry. The sequel shows that
Clavel was right as to where to look for your thief and your goods
when you have been robbed. Evelyn wasted no time on Bromley or
Croydon. He went to London next day, and had five hundred
tickets printed, announcing what he had lost. The footpads were
not caught, but within two days all that he had lost, except his
sword, was recovered from the people who had, innocently or not,
bought them.

Clavel's warning to travellers not to travel on Sunday was hardly
necessary. The law at that time forbade Sunday travelling to carters,
drovers, chapmen and higglers. It was not forbidden to the general
public (except Roman Catholics) but the general public, for the most
part, imposed the ban themselves. Travelling on the Lord's day was
held to be a desecration, and nobody, if it could be avoided, travelled
on that day, for fear of some visitation. Ralph Thoresby, the antiquary, who was always on the road, records in his *Diary* two occasions
when he ignored the ban. On the first occasion, nothing happened
to him:

Constrained utterly against my mind to travel from Royston to Stamford, though the Lord's day; but either do so, or be left upon the road about a hundred miles from home and not knowing a foot of the way. . . . From Tuxford home: all along having large experience of the goodness of God in preservation from so many evils as might justly have befallen me.

On the second occasion, while Thoresby, the author of the sin, escaped without punishment, the visitation (in two doses) fell upon an innocent person who was merely acting under his orders. It fell upon the maid:

Thence rid to Newark: the maid unfortunately got a grievous fall; perhaps we may read the crime, travelling upon the Lord's day, in the punishment. . . . Thence to Wansford, near which town a cart driving furiously down the hill, hit the maid's horse and caught hold of her clothes, but got her not under the wheel, though at the very door of death.

Clavel does not appear in either the Newgate Calendar or Johnson's *Lives of the Highwaymen*, though his work was freely used by other pamphleteers. Some fifty years after his *Recantation* was published, a prose version was issued, without acknowledgment to him, purporting to be the confession of a highwayman of a later time. It contains one or two hints not given by Clavel; for example:

Having taken a solemn oath to be true one to another, their next business is to acquaint themselves by tapsters, hostlers, chamberlains, or others, what booties are stirring, how contained, and whither bound. . . . In the first place, you must have variety of periwigs planted in your lodgings; and the like you must carry abroad, if occasion require the necessity of changing the colour of your hair; neither must you be without your false beards of several colours; for want of them, you may cross your locks athwart your mouth, which is a good disguise; patches contribute much thereto.

But for the most part it follows his work point by point. For some reason he is less known than the rest of that seventeenth-century constellation of tobymen—Thomas Witherington, Isaac Atkinson (a pleasant rogue who robbed only lawyers), James Hind, Philip Stafford, Claude du Vall, Richard Dudley, William Nevison (of the ride to York), James Whitney, John Cottington (known, from his favourite drink, as "Mulled Sack"), William Davis ("the Golden Farmer") and Old Mob, who once robbed Bloody Jeffreys.

All these men, especially du Vall, have been over-romanticised in their biographies or pseudo-biographies. They may have been dashing and courageous figures, but most of the pleasant stories about them have the air of having been born in the fancy of the hacks who compiled the records of picaresquerie. There are authentic accounts of many of them galloping away when faced with resistance; and equally attested accounts of ruffianly behaviour not only to men but to women. Evelyn mentions a robbery on a Hertfordshire road of Government servants bringing in tax-money from the north. While some of the gang attended to the securing of the money, others stopped all travellers passing either way, dismounted them, and carried them into a field under guard, until the job was done. When everything was secured, they killed the horses of those they had dismounted, including the horses of the Government servants, so that there should be no pursuit, and rode away. They left behind them sixteen people with sixteen dead horses.

The one pleasant trait about the tobyman was that he was no skinflint. His attitude to money was easy come, easy go, and fill the pipe and can. He spent freely, treating all comers, and no doubt the graceful legends that gathered about him came from the less particular poor who had profited from his hospitality at the tavern or the inn, and could overlook his obstreperous manners. But to the traveller of those times he was not romantic and not very fearsome. He was just an ugly nuisance.

Perhaps the most famous journey of this century was that crisscross, fugitive journey of delays and suspense and narrow escapes, made in the autumn of 1651 by a young man just turned twenty-one; the journey from Worcester to Shoreham. It occupied nearly six weeks, and during that time Prince Charles was moving back and forth in a certain area of England, with Cromwell's troopers all round him. Sometimes he stayed at an inn where they were quartered; sometimes he passed on the road through a whole regiment; sometimes he was suspected and pursued; once he was taken for one of themselves, and joined a discussion on what ought to be done to "the rogue, Charles Stuart." Why he escaped when so many in those parts knew him, and a price of a thousand pounds was put upon him, is one of those mysteries. Twice a ship was got ready for him, and twice he was disappointed; once at Lyme, by the captain's wife hearing of the proposed trip and locking the captain in his bedroom; and once at Southampton, by the ship being commandeered for troop-carrying to the Channel Isles. As for tight corners, during that six weeks he was in a score of them, but against all reason and probability, he came through. His escape was indeed as most of the Boscobel Tracts call it on their title-pages—Miraculous. As Thomas Blount says, in his *Boscobel*:

From the 3 of September at Worcester to the 15 of October at Bright-thelmston, being one and forty days, he passed through more dangers than he traveiled miles, of which yet he traversed in that time only neer three hundred . . . sometimes on foot with uneasy shoes; at other times on horseback, encumbered with a portmanteau and which was worse, at another time, on the gall-back'd slow paced miller's horse; sometimes acting one disguise in course linnen and a leather doublet; sometimes another of almost as bad a complection; one day he is forced to sculk in a barn at Madely; another day sits with Colonel Carlos in a tree, with his feet extremely surbated, and at night glad to lodge with William Penderel in a secret place at Boscobel which never was intended for the dormitory of a King. Sometimes he was forced to shift with course fare for a belly-full; another time in a wood, glad to relieve the necessities of nature with a messe of milk served up in an homely dish by good-wife Yates, a poor countrywoman. Then again for a variety of tribulation, when he thought himself almost out of danger, he directly meets some of those rebels, who so greedily sought his bloud, yet by God's providence had not the power to discover him.

The journey touched ten counties. The erratic route, owing to change of mind, or breakdown of plans, or the presence of the enemy, was: Worcester, Stourbridge, Whiteladies, Madeley, Boscobel, Moseley, Bentley Hall, Bromsgrove, Stratford-on-Avon, Long Marston, Chipping Campden, Cirencester, Bristol, Abbot's Leigh, Castle Cary, Trent (near Sherborne), Charmouth, Bridport, Broad-windsor, back to Trent, Wincanton, Mere, Heale House (near Salisbury), Stonehenge, Warnford, Broad-Halfpenny Down, Hamble-don, Arundel, Bramber, Brighton, Shoreham. There were periods of rest, when he was lodged in priests' holes or other secret chambers of his entertainers, but most of those forty-one days were a test of almost superhuman endurance. Whatever he may have been as monarch, he was gallant enough as prince.

In 1680 he dictated to Pepys an account of his Worcester wander-ings, and an excellent travel narrative it makes. Its casual tone, whether describing the hospitality he enjoyed, or startling encounters with the troopers, or hurried flights from this or that place, gives it a special piquancy. There was the occasion at Bridport, when he found the town full of Cromwell's men, and yet went among them as "Will Jackson," manservant, groomed his master's horses, dined, stayed about two hours, and then rode away with his master through a crowded street:

So Frank Windham, and Mrs. Coningsby and I went in the morning, on horse-back, away to Bridport; and just as we came into the town, I could see the streets full of red-coats, Cromwell's soldiers, being a regiment of Colonel Haynes, namely fifteen hundred men going to embark to take Jersey, at which Frank Windham was very much startled, and asked me what I would do? I told him that we must go impudently into the best inn in the town, and take a chamber there, as the only thing to be done: because we should otherwise miss my Lord Wilmot, in case we went any-where else. . . . So we rode directly into the best inn of the place, and found the yard very full of soldiers. I alighted, and taking the horses thought it the best way to go blundering in among them, and lead them through the middle of the soldiers into the stable, which I did; and they were very angry with me for my rudeness.

After the Restoration, and with quieter times, the "tour" became a thing to do. Diaries and letters of the period contain records of many a tour, and *Descriptions* of England increased; among them Drayton's *Poly-olbion*, in alexandrines; a work which few people have read even once, while thousands can repeat his sonnet, "Since there's no help, come let us kiss and part. . . ." To meet this new interest, the first really useful road-book appeared—Ogilby's *Britannia* (1675). This was one more Description, but its value to travellers lay in its strip-maps of main roads, showing routes and mileage, bridges, hills, streams, forests, and the direction of each by-road. It was the first thing of its kind that got anywhere near accuracy. Ogilby went over each main road with a dimensurator—a wheel fitted with a ten-mile length of cord—and every stretch of road was surveyed under his personal direction. His work soon became indispensable, and it served many generations until it was superseded by the later works of Cary, Paterson, and Mogg.

Pepys and Evelyn followed the touring fashion of their time, though neither made many journeys. Others were Sir William Dugdale, James Brome, Ralph Thoresby, Celia Fiennes. Dugdale, Thoresby and Celia Fiennes have much to say about their travelling experiences, but Brome's book is little more than a gossiping gazeteer. He talks only of places, merely saying "We arrived at Bath . . ." —"Next morning we went on to Gloucester." He says nothing about the actual travelling; what means they used or what route they followed, and nothing of the incident of road or inn. He was a parson, and concerned with edifying his readers, and no doubt considered the details of travel to be mere vanities.

Evelyn, like many Englishmen, had made the Grand Tour of Europe before it occurred to him to take a look at his own country. He did this only after his marriage. His impressions of the tour are recorded in the *Diary*, and some of them are piquant. He set out in June 1654. He did not possess such a luxury as Lord Henry Howard's "flying chariot with six horses" in which he rode some years later, but he did have a coach of his own and four horses. The tour was a roundabout affair of 700 miles, taking in the West, the Midlands, Yorkshire, Lincolnshire, and down to London and his home at Deptford.

At Marlborough he found nothing observable except the Mount, which "seems to have been cast up by hand." At Bath he notes that "the town is built intirely of stone, but the streets narrow, uneven, and unpleasant." At Bristol he saw "the manner of refining sugar and casting it into loaves, where we had a collation of eggs fried in the sugar furnace together with excellent Spanish wine; but what was most stupendous to me was the rock of St. Vincent, a little distance from the town. . . . Here we went searching for diamonds." At Oxford, his own university, he found everything good, and was as sentimental and uncritical as any old-school-tie wearer of to-day. From Oxford he turned back westward, and experienced a touch of country hospitality not wholly agreeable. "In the meantime our coachmen were made so exceedingly drunk that in returning home we escaped great dangers. This it seems was by order of the Knight, that all gentlemen's servants be so treated; but the custom is a barbarous one." The streets of Salisbury he found "negligently kept" and "the common buildings are despicable and the streets are dirty."

After seeing Stonehenge and Devizes, he went on to Gloucester, and from there to Worcester "by a way thick-planted with cider fruit." He climbed to the top of the Malvern Hills, and enjoyed the prospect which tourists of to-day enjoy over twelve counties. From Worcester he went to Warwick, and went over the castle; and then to Coventry; and into Leicestershire and Rutland. Uppingham was "pretty and well built of stone, which is a rarity in that part of England, where most of the rural parishes are but of mud, and the people living as wretchedly as in the most impoverished parts of France, which they much resemble, being idle and sluttish. The country much in common; the gentry free drinkers."

Leicester he calls "the old and ragged City of Leicester, large and pleasantly seated, but despicably built." He then went north by Oakham, Stamford, Newark, Nottingham, Sherwood Forest, Mansfield, Worksop, and Doncaster—"famous for great wax-lights and good stockings." Then to York, and on to Beverley, where he was shown the church by a woman 100 years old, who "spake the language of Queen Mary's days in whose time she was born." From Beverley he went to Hull, and then across the Humber in a barge and on to Brigg ("famous for the plantations of licorice") and so to Lincoln, "an old confused town, very long, uneven, steep and ragged."

From Lincoln he cut across to Grantham, then through Northamptonshire to Peterborough, and on to Cambridge. Cambridge, of course, was not so good as Oxford. "Trinity College is said by some to be the fairest quadrangle of any University in Europe, but in truth is far inferior to that of Christ Church in Oxford." The Library of King's was "too narrow." Catherine Hall was "a mean structure." Jesus College was "one of the best built, but in a melancholy situation." The schools were "very despicable," and the Public Library "but mean." The whole town was set "in a low, dirty, unpleasant place, the streets ill paved, the air thick and infected by the Fennes, nor are its churches anything considerable in compare with those of Oxford." And so from Cambridge to Audley End, Bishop's Stortford and London. Nowhere in his account of the tour does he mention bad roads, perhaps because they were so usual that he thought them not worth mentioning, or perhaps because his coach was better sprung than most.

Pepys found bad roads on almost all his journeys, and, what was perhaps worse to him, as a practising musician, bad music. It was still the custom that travellers, on arriving at their inns, should be welcomed by the town's music, and be farewell'd with a flourish of it; but it was seldom worth the money. "The poor, as they did yesterday, did stand at the coach to have something given them, as they do to all great persons; and I did give them something; and the town music did also come and play; but Lord! what sad music they made!" . . . That was at Cambridge. At Reading it was sadder. "Rose, and paying the reckoning, 12s. 6d.; servants and poor, 2s. 6d.; music, the worst we have had, coming to our chamber-door, but calling us by wrong names." Another custom among travellers was that of giving donations to the road-menders. On two occasions during a journey to and from Bath, he mentions distributing money to "menders of the highway."

On a journey across the Fens he speaks of having his horse almost "sink to the belly." The way from Brampton to Baldock was "very bad." The road between Finchley and Barnet was "torn, plowed and digged up." One of the worst stretches, along which he often travelled, was the Hertfordshire road—Hoddesdon–Ware–Puckeridge–Buntingford. This was not only ill-kept, but whenever rains made the rivers rise, it was flooded. Sometimes, for weeks, it was useless; neither coach nor even horse could find a passage, and by-roads had to be used.

After long complaint, permission was given to the local authorities to collect tolls from users of the road by which a fund could be created for its repair; and thus began the system which was maintained even into our own century. That particular stretch of road was known to and dreaded by all regular travellers. Late in the century, Thoresby speaks of it as a pleasant road in summer, and very bad in winter, because of the depth of the cart-ruts, though not, he says, as bad as the stretch to Puckeridge and Buntingford, and part of the way to Royston. His description of a journey along it in wet weather shows that it was not only a bad road but dangerous to the point of fatality:

> Morning, rode by Puckeridge to Ware, where we baited, and had some showers, which raised the washes upon the road to that height that passengers from London that were upon the road swam, and a poor higgler was drowned, which prevented our travelling for many hours, yet towards evening adventured with some country people, who conducted us . . . over the meadows, whereby we missed the deepest of the Wash at Cheshunt, though we rode to the saddle-skirts for a considerable way, but got safe to Waltham Cross, where we lodged. Morning, rode by Edmunton (where we had our horses led about a mile over the deepest of the Wash) to Highgate, and thence to London. I have the greatest cause of thankfulness, for the goodness of my heavenly protector, that being exposed to greater dangers by my horse's boggling at every coach and waggon we met, I received no damage, though the ways were very bad, the ruts deep, and the roads extremely full of water, which rendered my circumstances (often meeting the loaded waggons in very inconvenient places) not only melancholy, but really very dangerous.

An idle traveller of the seventeenth century, who went out to see:

> Bridges, fountaines, mountaines, valleis,
> Cauls, cells, hillocks, high-wayes, shallows,
> Paths, towns, villages, and trenches;
> Chast-choice-chary, merry wenches. . . .

was that odd creation whose creator cannot certainly be named— "Drunken Barnaby." He went on horseback, and seems to have travelled in many parts of England in what we would describe to-day as one long pub-crawl. The work, *Drunken Barnaby's Four Journeys to the North of England*, was written originally in Latin, and translated into doggerel English verse. The general effect, both of the verse and of the carousals it reports, is one of headache. The first journey took him to Banbury, Oxford, Leicester, Nottingham, Doncaster, Bradford, Keighley, and on to the Lakes. The second was from Lancaster to London by way of Preston, Warrington,

Lichfield, Coventry, Towcester, Dunstable, St. Albans. The third was from Islington through Ware, Cambridge, Wansford, Stamford, Bawtry, York, Thirsk, Darlington, and across country to Kendal and the Lakes again. The fourth "journey" consisted of a series of short North country visits.

In coach travelling little improvement was made, either in the coaches themselves or in their speed. Various attempts were made

A Seventeenth-Century Sedan Chair

towards coaches of lighter structure, but it was apparently not easy to get lightness combined with the strength necessary to the roads of that time. Pepys describes a new coach designed by a friend of his:

> After dinner comes Colonel Blunt in his new chariot made with springs; as that was of wicker, wherein a while since we rode at his house. And he hath rode, he says, now his journey, many miles in it with one horse, and out-drives any coach, and out-goes any horse, and so easy, he says. So for curiosity I went into it to try, and up the hill to the heath, and over the cart-ruts and found it pretty well, but not so easy as he pretends.

Heavy and slow remained the rule. As late as 1683 the journey from York to London was still five days. The night halts were Doncaster, Newark, Stamford, and Stevenage. From London to York the coach dined at Welwyn, and slept at Biggleswade; dined at Huntingdon, slept at Stamford; dined at Newark, slept at Barnby Moor; dined at Doncaster, slept at Ferrybridge, and was at York the next day. Those journeys were made by Ralph Thoresby; the first coach journeys he had made; and he made them with some hesitation:

> Up pretty timely, preparing for a journey, and somewhat concerned about company, fearful of being confined to a coach for so many days with unsuitable persons, and not one that I know of.

The company, however, was not too bad. At the first stop, they "took up a gentleman and his man, who proved very good company, not so hot as I feared, being the Archbishop's son, Richard Sterne, Esq., Parliament man for Ripon." The comment is a little cryptic to us of to-day; we have another meaning for "not so hot," and the comfort he drew from "Archbishop's son" is not now comprehensible. But it appears that coach company was less offensive than he had anticipated. Snobbery in all matters was as much abroad then as now. It seems necessary to a certain type of the human creature that he should always be in a position to "look down" upon other creatures. In travelling, as in other phases of life, there were ranks and dignities. The lord with his "flying chariot" looked down upon the squire with his coach and four. The squire looked down upon the horseman. The horseman looked down upon coach travellers. Coach travellers looked down upon those poor people who travelled by the stage-waggon. And those in the stage-waggon looked down upon the still poorer who plodded their way on foot.

The dangers of travel were so much recognised that any man going a journey could, on request to the vicar of his parish, have prayers offered for his safety. Thoresby once had this done, and was ridiculed by two of his fellow townsmen; but, as he pointed out, "how piteous a case are we in, who, being exposed to continual dangers, and have so many instances of such as never return home, one merchant of this town lately cast away . . . and yet cannot desire the prayers for the merciful protection of God, but must be ridiculed, not by the commonalty only, but even by such as pretend to be zealots in religion." Most travellers, however, took a chance; and it may be that Thoresby, just because he was always thinking of the perils of travel, and seeking protection against them, fell into rather more of them than the average traveller. The apprehensive usually get a larger share of trouble than the reckless.

Misson, another French visitor, wrote some *Memoirs and Observations* on our manners and customs, and speaks of our modes of travel, but says nothing of any dangers:

They have several ways of travelling in England. The post is under a good regulation throughout, and the horses are better than those of France. There are coaches that go to all the great towns by moderate journeys, and others, which they call Flying Coaches, that will travel twenty leagues a day or more; but these don't go to all places. They have no *Messageries de Chevaux*, as in France; but you may hire horses for what time you please. The sea and the rivers also furnish their respective conveniences for travelling. I say nothing of the waggons, which are great carts, covered in, that lumber along but very heavily; only a few poor old women make use of this vehicle.

In his comment on the stage-waggons he was not quite accurate; they were used, as I have said, by the poorer people of all sorts. A mode in use at the time, which he does not mention, was the pannier —two deep baskets slung on either side of a horse. These panniers were generally used for carrying goods, but on occasion, when a family was travelling, the children rode in them. They were introduced in the late seventeenth century, and in some parts of the country they survived into the present century. On Exmoor, in 1925, I have seen countrywomen going to market on horseback, with panniers.

Misson speaks of travel by sea and river, but while this mode was frequently used, as we may see from guides and directories, few travellers left any record of their journeys in this way. On the Thames, boats plied as far up as Oxford and as far down as the Estuary; and there was a service of coastal wherries to all busy ports on the east and south. They carried both goods and passengers, and went up all the important rivers—the Medway, Orwell, Avon, Severn, Humber, Ouse, etc. John Taylor, early in the century, made two or three journeys by water, and wrote an account of two of them—one from London to York, and one from London to Salisbury, entitled respectively *A Merry-Wherry-Ferry Voyage* and *A Discovery by Sea*. Each voyage took about a month, and as he took his turn with the oars, he found his sea and river journeys more full of "toil, travail, and danger" than any of his road journeys.

It was the slowness of water travel, rather than its dangers, that gave it so little custom. Those to whom time was a consideration kept to the horse and the road, though the roads were still not what the King's highways should be. In the less frequented parts they were entirely neglected, and those in constant use, however often repaired, were within a few weeks torn up by the lumbering carts and waggons. The only occasion, in his book of *Travels*, when James Brome makes any reference to the conditions of travel is when he speaks of the roads in Derbyshire, which he does in rather curious terms. The bogs and the rocks in that country "annoy" the roads, and the roads themselves are "very cross" and "irksome." In Cotton's continuation of *The Compleat Angler*, Derbyshire roads are presented as highly dangerous to the inexperienced. Somewhere near Ashbourne, Piscator encounters Viator, who asks him the way to that town, and complains of the length of the Derbyshire miles and of the "foul ways." Piscator asks his destination:

Viator: 'Tis into Lancashire, sir; and about some business of concern to a near relation of mine; for I assure you I do not use to take such long journeys as from Essex upon the single account of pleasure.

Piscator: From thence, sir! I do not then wonder you should appear dissatisfied with the length of the miles and the foulness of the way: though I am sorry you should begin to quarrel with them so soon; for believe me, sir, you will find the miles much longer, and the way much worse, before you come to your journey's end.

Piscator invites him to his home, and on the way Viator is much troubled by the steep descents and the flimsy bridges:

Viator: I think it is the strangest place that ever, sure, men and horses went down; and that (if there be any safety at all) the safest way is to alight.

Piscator: I think so, too, for you, who are mounted upon a beast not acquainted with these slippery stones; and though I frequently ride down, I will alight, too, to bear you company. . . .

Viator: Would I were well down, though! Hoist thee! there's one fair escape! these stones are so slippery I cannot stand! yet again! I think I were best lay my heels in my neck and tumble down.

Piscator: If you think your heels will defend your neck, that is the way to be soon at the bottom; but give me your hand at this broad stone, and then the worst is past.

Viator: I thank you, sir, I am now past it, I can go myself. What's here the sign of a bridge? Do you use to travel with wheelbarrows in this country?

Piscator: Not that I ever saw, sir. Why do you ask that question?

Viator: Because this bridge certainly was made for nothing else; why, a mouse can hardly go over it; 'tis not two fingers broad.

Piscator: You are pleasant, and I am glad to see you so: but I have rid over the bridge many a dark night.

Viator: Let me tell you, I would not ride over it for a thousand pounds, nor fall off it for two; and yet I think I dare venture on foot, though if you were not by to laugh at me, I should do it on all fours.

Piscator: Well, sir, your mirth becomes you, and I am glad to see you safe over; and now you are welcome into Staffordshire.

Viator: I hope we have no more of these Alps to pass over.

Piscator: No, no, sir; only this ascent before you, which you see is not very easy. . . .

Viator: Well, if ever I come to London (of which many a man there, if he were in my place, would make a question) I will sit down and write my travels. . . . Pray, what do you call this hill we came down?

Piscator: We call it Hanson Toot.

Viator: Why, farewell Hanson Toot! I'll no more on thee. I'll go twenty miles about first.

Other references to bad roads are made in another thing of Cotton's—his *Journey to Ireland*; an amusing sketch, in rather ambling

F

verse, of the various aspects of travel, its pleasures and perils and encounters. Distinguished travellers, that is, travellers well-dressed and with some equipage, were often waited upon, at their inns, by the mayor of the town. Cotton records that he was twice waited upon in this way, and each time he and the mayor sat up tippling. He had to hire a guide to make his way from Chester, over the mountains, to Conway, and complains of the high price—twenty shillings and his charges on the road.

By his style of travelling, a man showed his rank. In some cases it was the only chance he had of showing it to the general public, since few men, however noble, were known outside their own neighbourhood. Perhaps, therefore, men of that time may be forgiven for trying, by rather vulgar display, to make their rank appear a little higher than it was. The nobility usually travelled with outriders and a bodyguard of servants, making a show not only of pomp but of force. Some of those attendants were really necessary. Even the best coaches could not always be trusted to stand up to those rutted or pot-holed roads, and often there was a breakage of some vital part, or an overturning or ditching. Every coach, private and public, carried a box of tools for repairs, and among the entourage of the lords there would always be a blacksmith and a wheelwright. To restore an overturned coach, or to lift it out of a ditch or swamp, needed the services of three or four very strong men; the coaches of that time were nothing like the light mail-coaches of the early nineteenth century.

In addition to outriders, the lords also travelled with running footmen, who went ahead of the coach on foot, as heralds to announce the coming of the mighty, and get the way cleared. They wore the livery of the family, with a sort of jockey-cap, and carried long staves, and were specially selected for their ability to run at a jog-trot for half a day at a time. The head of their staves was a hollow ball which carried liquid refreshment. Their office is commemorated in the sign of an old Mayfair public-house.

When Evelyn accompanied one of our ambassadors to Dover, the procession was composed of four coaches, three waggons, and forty horsemen. They took three days on the journey, and at Dover the ambassador was driven in his coach down to the beach, and into the sea to the waiting boats which took them off to the yacht. Another mode of end-of-the-century travelling—that of the country squire showing his consequence—is presented in Vanbrugh's *Journey to London*:

James: Sir, Sir, do you hear the news? they are all a coming.
Uncle James: Ay sirrah, I hear it, with a pox to it.

James: Sir, here's John Moody arrived already; he's stumping about the streets in his dirty boots, and asking every man he meets if they can tell where he may have a good lodging for a parliament man . . . he tells them his lady and all the family are coming too, and that they are so nobly attended, they care not a fig for anybody. Sir, they have added two cart-horses to the four old geldings, because my lady will have it said, she came to town in her coach and six, and heavy George the plowman rides postillion.

Uncle Richard: The Lord have mercy upon all good folks! what work these people will make! Dost know when they'll be here?

James: John says, Sir, they'd have been here last night, but that the old wheezy-belly horse tired, and the two fore-wheels came crash down at once in Waggonrut Lane. Sir, they were cruelly loaden, as I understand, my lady herself, he says, laid on four mail-trunks, besides the great deal-box; which fat Tom sat upon behind. . . . Then within the coach there was Sir Francis, my Lady, the great fat lap-dog, Squire Humphry, Miss Betty, my lady's maid Mrs. Handy and Doll Tripe the cook. . . .

Uncle Richard: Very well. . . .

James: Then for band-boxes, they were so bepiled up to Sir Francis's nose, that he could only peep out at a chance hole with one eye, as if he were viewing the country through a perspective glass. . . .

For protection against highwaymen they carried the family basket-hilt sword, a Turkish scimitar, an old blunderbuss, a bag of bullets, and a horn of gunpowder. As provision against faintness between inns, they carried baskets of plum-cake, Dutch gingerbread, Cheshire cheese, Naples biscuits, macaroons, neats'-tongues, and cold boiled beef; with bottles of usquebaugh, black-cherry brandy, cinnamon-water, sack, tent, and strong beer.

A series of hurried journeys with little pomp about them were those back-and-forth journeys of indecision, and fright, and second thoughts, made in 1688 by James II. After some weeks of fumbling with the question of the arrival of the Prince of Orange, at three o'clock in the morning of December 10th, without disclosing his plans to Parliament, he went off secretly and in disguise with Sir Edward Hales. They went down the river to a fishing-boat which was to carry them to France, and they might have got right away without second thoughts, but that the boat had to put in to Faversham for ballast. There they were boarded by some armed fishermen who were hunting for escaping Papists. They took from James his sword and his money—three hundred guineas; all he had—but when they learned who he was they restored them and treated him with more civility. They took him ashore, where he became the spectacle of the town—"when he who had ruled three kingdoms and might have been the arbiter of all Europe, was now in such mean hands, and so low an equipage." He was, in fact, arrested, and kept something of a prisoner; but when the Prince of Orange heard of his arrest he sent certain lords to see that James was unharmed and to assure him that he was free to go where he would.

The Privy Council wanted him back in London, and accordingly the general of the King's army was sent down with coaches and guards to bring him back. He was received by the people with acclamation, and decided to send to the prince, who was at Windsor, and invite him to Whitehall for a consultation. The Prince declined the meeting, and in his message stated that he himself was coming to London, and that it would be better that James should withdraw. Since this amounted to an order, James once again left Whitehall Palace, with bag and baggage, and again went down the river, this time to Rochester, under the guard of the Prince's men, but under no restraint of movement. While he was at Rochester, where he stayed a week, he was visited by numbers of adherents who wanted him to stay, while his own inclination, remembering what had happened to his father, was to go. Between the two, he could come to no decision.

At last he made an unexpected, and final, visit to London, on a Sunday, and, according to Evelyn, "goes to masse, and dines in public, a Jesuit saying grace. I was present." On that night he held a Council, refused to assent to their proposals, and once more, this time irrevocably, went to Rochester. "I saw the King take barge to Gravesend at 12 o'clock—a sad sight!" On Christmas Eve he left Rochester in great secrecy and passed over to France. News was still so slow in passing that in some parts of the remote North they knew nothing of the change until three months after it was accomplished.

The "romance" of the road, with which novelists have made so many effects, appears scarcely at all in fact. Most of what has been presented as the "romance" was truly only discomfort. Curled and booted highwaymen, dancing corantos with fair ladies on Hounslow Heath, make pretty pictures; but few if any travellers ever witnessed anything of the kind. There were, of course, elopements by moonlight, and the occasional abduction of an heiress; but they were few. The search for anything of a really romantic nature brings little result; though Evelyn does record one passionate episode, with the highway as its setting, which he himself witnessed. It happened during a journey from Northampton, which he describes as "a journey of adventures and knight-errantry," since two love-affairs were going on among the company—one of the high world and one of the low.

A young man, who later became Privy Purse to the Duke of York, was deeply and bitterly in love with one Dorothy Howard, a Maid of Honour. The mother of Dorothy would not consider him, and he went to Evelyn for advice. Evelyn "could not but pitty them both," and pleaded the young man's cause to the mother, but without effect. Thus on that journey there were two broken hearts among the better sort, and a third, as appeared later, among the servants. This was the heart of a young man, one of Dorothy Howard's servants, in whom emotionalism ran high:

> One of the lady's servants being as desperately in love with Mrs. Howard's woman as Mr. Graham was with her daughter, and she riding on horseback behind his rival, the amorous and jealous youth having a little drink in his pate, had here killed himself had he not been prevented; for, alighting from his horse, and drawing his sword, he endeavoured twice or thrice to fall on it, but was interrupted by our coachman and a stranger passing by. After this, running to his rival and snatching his sword from his side (for we had beaten his own out of his hand) and on the sudden pulling down his mistress, would have run both of them through; we parted them, but not without some blood. This miserable creature poisoned himself for her not many days after they came to London.

In the latter years of the century, tolls for bridges, causeways, ferries, and certain roads increased rapidly, and the system of toll-gates, which hampered travellers for the next two centuries, was introduced. Tolls, as mentioned earlier, were payable by all vehicles on the highways of the Home Counties, which bore the heaviest traffic; though the roads were not barred or in any way obstructed. But as the speed of travel increased, it seems that some travellers were able to dash past the collector without paying; so in 1695 a new law was made giving local authorities the power to block the main road with a turnpike; a term which, in the nineteenth century, was synonymous with main road. A turnpike was a defensive barrier of pikes fastened to a frame which stretched across the road. When the traveller had paid his toll, the frame turned on a central pivot, and made a clear way. In the eighteenth century it was replaced by the ordinary toll-gate. With the turnpike came two essentials of travel which, until then, had been unknown to travellers: the milestone and the signpost.

CHAPTER THREE

Georgian Journeys

THE SPEED of the public coaches of the early eighteenth century was not that of private coaches. Travellers of those days were familiar with coach-bills which announced the performance of Flying

YORK Four Days Stage-Coach.

Begins on Friday the 12th of April 1706

ALL that are desirous to pass from London to York, or from York to London or any other Place on that Road: Let them Repair to the Black Swan in Holbourn in London and to the Black Swan in Coney-street in York

At both which Places they may be received in a Stage Coach every Monday, Wednesday and Friday, which performs the whole Journey in Four Days. (if God permits.) And sets forth at Five in the Morning.

And returns from York to Stamford in two days, and from Stamford by Huntington to London in two days more. And the like Stages on their return

Allowing each Passenger 14l. weight, and all above 3d. a Pound

Performed By { Benjamin Kingman
Henry Harrison.
Walter Baynes.

Also this gives Notice that Newcastle Stage Coach, sets out from York, every Monday, and Friday, and from Newcastle every Monday, and Friday

Rec.d in pt 05·00· o of Mr. Bodmafild for 5 p's for Monday the 3 of June 1706

A York Coaching Notice of 1706

Machines, but flying was only a term. A Flying Machine, with divine aid, could get from London to York in four days. It set out from Holborn every Monday, Wednesday, and Friday, and "performs the whole journey in Four Days (*if God permits*). And sets forth at Five in the Morning. And return from York to Stamford in two days, and from Stamford, by Huntingdon, to London in two days more." A journey to Chester by another "flier" took six days.

Even in the middle of the century, Birmingham was two and a half days travel from London. The coach set out at five o'clock every Thursday morning from Aldersgate, going via Aylesbury, Banbury, and Warwick, and reaching Birmingham on Saturday afternoon. This was a six-horse machine, and the announcement of two and a half days was made with a note of pride. Dover was a two-day journey; the coach dined at Rochester and slept at Canterbury. Manchester was four and a half days; Exeter, six days; Norwich, by the Expedition Coach, was two days; while in 1751 the owners of the Edinburgh stage-coach offered to perform the Edinburgh–London or London–Edinburgh journey in ten days in summer and twelve days in winter.

In those days, nobody enjoyed travelling in close company with strangers. There was then little communal spirit among the middle class, and complaints of the proximity of other people are frequent. Reading those complaints, one wonders what the writers would have had to say had they been born into a later age, and had to travel at six in the evening on a London tube-train. Steele, writing in 1711, expresses the general attitude to stage-coach travel:

> We were in some little time fixed in our seats, and sat with that dislike which people not too good-natured usually conceive of each other at first sight. The coach jumbled us insensibly into some sort of familiarity; and we had not moved above two miles, when the widow asked the Captain what success he had in his recruiting. The officer, with a frankness he believed very graceful, told her That indeed he had but very little luck, and had suffered much by desertion, therefore should be glad to end his warfare in the service of her or her fair daughter. . . . This was followed by a vain laugh of his own, and a deep silence of all the rest of the company. I had nothing left for it but to fall fast asleep.

A later remark in the essay—that one member of the company took it upon himself to see that the coachman upheld the right the coach had, as going to London, of taking place of all short-stage vehicles—shows that there were ranks and dignities in coaching. The difference between London-bound coaches and cross-country coaches was reflected in the attention shown at their inns. The opening scene of Farquhar's *Beaux Strategem* (1707) makes a point of this:

> *Boniface:* Chamberlain! Maid! Cherry! daughter Cherry! All asleep? All dead?

Cherry: Here! Here! Why d'ye bawl so, father? D'ye think we have no ears?

Boniface: You deserve to have none, you young minx. The company of the Warrington coach has stood in the hall this hour, and nobody to show them to their chambers.

Cherry: And let 'em wait, father; there's neither red-coat in the coach nor footman behind it.

Boniface: But they threaten to go to another inn to-night.

Cherry: That they dare not, for fear the coachman should overturn them to-morrow. Coming! Coming! Here's the London coach arrived. . . . Very welcome, gentlemen. Chamberlain, show the Lion and the Rose.

Swift, who disliked the company of other people in any circumstances, naturally disliked coach travel and the company it (literally) forced upon him. In a satirical sketch he describes a coach journey from Aldersgate to Chester. The coach left Aldersgate at three in the morning:

> Roused from sound sleep—thrice called—at length I rise,
> Yawning, stretch out my arm, half close my eyes;
> By steps and lanthorn enter the machine,
> And take my place—how cordially!—between
> Two aged matrons of excessive bulk,
> To mend the matter, too, of meaner folk;
> While in like mood, jammed in on t'other side,
> A bullying captain and a fair one ride,
> Foolish as fair, and in whose lap a boy—
> Our plague eternal, but her only joy.
> At last, the glorious number to complete,
> Steps in my landlord for that bodkin seat;
> When soon, by every hillock, rut and stone,
> Into each other's face by turns we're thrown.
> This grandam scolds, that coughs, the captain swears,
> The fair one screams and has a thousand fears;
> While our plump landlord, trained in other lore,
> Slumbers at ease nor yet ashamed to snore. . . .
> Sweet company! Next time, I do protest, sir,
> I'd walk to Dublin ere I'd ride to Chester.

Considering that the English had, by that time, become such great travellers, it is odd that they made so much fuss and complaint about it. The love of travel was running in their blood, and they could endure hardship as well as any; yet almost every account of English travel, up to the middle nineteenth century, is loaded with grumbles, so that one wonders why those travellers continued, often without necessity, to do something so obnoxious to them. But they did continue. All through the eighteenth century there were travellers who travelled to see what they could see. Thoresby, who

31 The Inn Yard

From the engraving by William Hogarth

32 A Small Town Coach of *ca.* 1720
From an engraving after Hayman

33 Sedan Chairs, *ca.* 1740

is fuller of complaints than any, went on travelling into the time of George I. Others who left records of their journeys were Defoe, William Gilpin, Arthur Young, James Murray, Dr. Johnson, George Beaumont, Thomas Twining, Jonas Hanway, Thomas Pennant, Mrs. Calderwood, Edward Daniel Clarke; and among the foreigners who looked over us and our countryside were Cèsar de Saussure, Marcel d'Archenholz, Carl Moritz, and Henry Meister.

Englishmen were beginning to learn of the fascination of their own country, and to realise that while travel in foreign countries is always refreshing and instructive, travel in one's own country may often afford more surprise, and, in some places, give the traveller the impression of seeing matters more "foreign" than anything he saw in France, Italy, or Spain. As Swift remarked—"in how few hours, with a swift horse, a man may come among a people as unknown to him as the Antipodes." Some of the travellers were, of course, extremely tedious in their narratives—notably George Beaumont, Esquire, and Capt. Disney, whose names appear on the title-page of *A New Tour thro' England in the Summers of 1765, 1766, and 1767*. Their work might easily have been compiled from the books of their contemporaries. It tells us nothing about their travels; it merely takes a number of counties, and, under the heading of the principal towns of each, gives a note of the buildings, business, and curiosities of the place.

Defoe, in the preface to the third volume of his *Tour thro' the Whole Island of Great Britain*, made in 1722, gives his own notion of how such books should be written. He is another who tells us little of his adventures or encounters on the road, and he seems to regard such trivialities as scarcely worthy a place. He mentions two acquaintances who travelled together over England, each making his own notes. One noted only things that specially interested him. The other kept an exact journal. Defoe's approval goes to the first:

> He that took minutes, did so only of some very significant things; the rest he trusted to his memory, which was so good that it enabled him to write a very useful account of his whole journey after his return. . . . The other gentleman's papers, which he called an exact *Journal* contained the following very significant heads:
>
> 1. The day of the month when he set out.
> 2. The names of the towns where they dined every day, and where they lodged at night.
> 3. The signs of the inns where they dined and lodged, with memorandums of which had good claret and which not.
> 4. The day of the month when he returned.

G

But with all respect to Defoe, that is just the kind of thing most of us like to find in travel books, and the lack of it makes Defoe's *Tour* somewhat arid. Only here and there does he give us something more than an account of trade and manufactures and paving and so on; as in his sharp picture of the Stourbridge Fair at Cambridge, which he holds to be not only the greatest in the nation, but in the world, surpassing those of Leipzig, Frankfort, Nuremberg, or Augsburg:

> To attend this Fair, and the prodigious conflux of people which come to it, there are sometimes no less than fifty hackney coaches, which come from London, and ply night and morning to carry the people to and from Cambridge; for there the gross of them lodge; nay, which is still more strange, there are wherries brought from London on waggons, to ply upon the little river Cam, and to row people up and down from the town and from the Fair. . . .
>
> It is not to be wondered at if the town of Cambridge cannot receive or entertain the numbers of people that come to this Fair; not Cambridge only but all the towns round are full; nay, the very barns and stables are turned into inns, and made as fit as they can to lodge the meaner sort of people; As for the people in the Fair, they all universally eat, drink, and sleep in their booths and tents; and the said booths are so intermingled with taverns, coffee-houses, drinking-houses, eating-houses, cooks' shops etc. and all in tents, too, and so many butchers and higglers from all the neighbouring counties come into the Fair every morning with beef, mutton, fowls, butter, bread, cheese, eggs and such things, and go with them from tent to tent, from door to door, that there's no want of any provisions of any kind, either dressed or undressed. In a word, the Fair is like a well-governed city.

He gives another lively bit in his description of his journey over Blackstone Edge from Rochdale. In Rochdale the weather was warm and calm; the time was August and harvesting was going on. But on Blackstone Edge it was snowing. As they reached the top, it became a blizzard, so that they could not keep their eyes open to watch the way; nor, he adds, would this have helped them, since there was no way—only a precipice on one side and uneven ground on the other. The horses showed uneasiness at the situation, and a spaniel they had with them howled and ran away. They were beginning to call to one another to turn back, when they experienced a phenomenon. In the middle of the snowstorm they heard a terrific clap of thunder, "the first that ever I heard in a storm of snow, or I hope ever shall; nor did we perceive any lightning to precede the thunder, as it naturally must." While they were considering how to get back to Rochdale, one of them cried that he had found a way forward:

There was indeed the face of a road on the north side of the hill . . . but it was a very frightful one, narrow and deep, with a hollow precipice on the right, from whence the water descending from the hills made a wide channel at the bottom which looked like the mouth of a river gaping to receive us. After we had gone a little way, the hollow on the right appeared deeper and deeper, so that we thought it best to alight, and lead our horses about a mile, though the violence of the wind and snow continuing made it both troublesome and dangerous. . . . At length we came to the bottom, when we found the hollow part, which I have mentioned as a precipice, was come level with us. As it turned to the left towards us, we found a brook running from it, which crossed our way to the north. When we were got over this brook, which, from the snow on the hills, was risen about knee deep, we saw a few poor houses, but no human creature; till we called at a door, to get directions of our way, and then we found, that though nobody was to be seen without doors, they were very full within.

A light-hearted tour of the time, offering no instruction to the reader, is that which a few friends made in 1732. It is recorded in *The Five Days' Peregrination.* The behaviour of the party seems to have been what one may call Hogarthian; the kind of behaviour shown in some of his more boisterous pictures.

They left the Bedford Coffee House in Covent Garden just after midnight, and took a boat to Billingsgate. There they hired a boat for Gravesend. They breakfasted at Gravesend, and walked to Rochester, where they dined on soles and flounders with crab sauce, a calf's heart stuffed, a roast leg of mutton and green peas, with beer and port. After dinner, the two leaders of the party played at hopscotch in the colonnade under the town hall, and they then walked to Chatham, where they bought and ate a bag of shrimps. On the next day, Sunday, they walked from Rochester to Upnor, where they bought some cockles. They had a hurried dinner at the Smack Inn, and afterwards "we had a battle royal with sticks, pebbles and ——" something too Hogarthian to mention in these days. Walking back from Hoo, they found that one of the party had rather wide pockets to his coat, so they kept behind him, and one by one dropped pebbles in, until he began to sag and complained of the hard road and of feeling tired. At a village called North Street they found a well filled to the brim, and had another battle with buckets of water. At Stock they ordered supper, and while waiting for it had another battle with sticks and stones. At seven, they returned to the inn and cleaned their clothes, and after supper they sat at the inn door, drinking punch, while one of them, who could draw, did their

G*

portraits. At bedtime the battle was resumed in the bedroom with wigs, stockings, and pillows.

On Monday they set out to walk to Sheerness, when one of them, who thought he knew a short cut, led them over a stile and took them two miles out of their way in mud. They managed to get back to the road, and reached the Isle of Grain, where at the Chequers they had salt pork, bread, butter, buns and malt liquor, followed by another battle. And so on for three more days.

Who were the five who made this five-days' trip? The pamphlet reads like an account of the doings of five mindless apprentices. Actually, the party was led by two artists—William Hogarth and Samuel Scott. The others were John Thornhill, heir to Sir James Thornhill, Hogarth's father-in-law; John Tothall, a merchant; and Edward Forrest, an attorney.

Most travellers continued to speak bitterly about the state of the roads. Squire Western's sister held that it must be the scores of turnpike acts that were making them worse than they had been. Those of Sussex and Lancashire were specially picked out for condemnation. When, in 1703, Prince George of Denmark visited Petworth, the last stage of the journey—nine miles—took six hours. One member of the entourage stated that during fourteen hours, the time of the journey from London, he did not once alight from his horse except when the coach overturned or was ditched. "Almost every mile was signalised by the overturn of a carriage, or its temporary swamping in the mire. Even the royal chariot would have fared no better than the rest, had it not been for relays of peasants who poised and kept it erect by strength of arm."

Even as late as the middle of the century, Horace Walpole found the Sussex roads primeval. Writing to George Montagu, he says:

> If you love good roads, conveniences, good inns, plenty of postillions and horses, be so kind as never to go into Sussex. We thought ourselves in the northest part of England; the whole country has a Saxon air, and the inhabitants are savage, as if king George the second was the first monarch of the East Angles. Coaches grow there no more than balm and spices; we were forced to drop our post-chaise, that resembled nothing so much as harlequin's calash, which was occasionally a chaise or a baker's cart. We journeyed over Alpine mountains, drenched in clouds. . . . Sussex is a great damper of curiosities.

As for the roads of Lancashire, Thoresby specially warned travellers against them. He spoke of passing, in a stretch of only a few miles, a whole string of carts and waggons collapsed or ditched. Yet De Saussure, who visited us in 1725, and whose letters were translated in 1902 under the title of *A Foreign View of England in the Reigns of George I and George II* (John Murray), speaks of our roads as being "magnificent, wide, smooth, and well-kept." If he found them so good when most English travellers found them so bad, then the roads of France must have been unspeakable.

The genial and nonchalant John Gay, in his versified account of his five-days' ride to Exeter, made no complaint about roads or about any other incident of the journey. He was one of those who are always willing to be pleased, and his *Journey to Exeter* is written with an accent of delight. The road took them through Kensington, Hammersmith, Turnham Green, Brentford, Staines, each of which places is noted; and at Staines they crossed the river by ferry because the Staines bridge had been broken down by flood. And then:

> Prepared for war, now Bagshot Heath we cross,
> Where broken gamesters oft repair their loss.
> At Hartley Row the foaming bit we prest,
> While the fat landlord welcomed every guest.
> Supper was ended, healths the glasses crowned,
> Our host extolled his wine at every round,
> Relates the Justices' late meeting there,
> How many bottles drank, and what their cheer.

He slept the night at Hartley Row, and next evening reached Stockbridge. On the third day he crossed Salisbury Plain, dined at Salisbury, and at sunset reached Blandford. Next day, by way of Dorchester and Bridport, he got to Morecomlake, and dined on lobster, and inned for the night at Axminster. There he encountered something that has a rather modern note. In our own time we have been familiar with the "lady barber"; she was introduced as something of a novelty. But the early eighteenth century seems to have known her and taken her for granted:

> The maid, subdued by fees, her trunk unlocks,
> And gives the cleanly aid of dowlas smocks.
> Meantime our shirts her busy fingers rub,
> While the soap lathers o'er the foaming tub.
> If women's gear such pleasing dreams incite,
> Lend us your smocks, ye damsels, every night.
> We rise; our beards demand the barber's art;
> A female enters, and performs the part.
> The weighty golden chain adorns her neck,
> And three gold rings her skilful hand bedeck;
> Smooth o'er our chins her easy fingers move,
> Soft as when Venus stroked the beard of Jove.

The fifth day brought him to Honiton and, by evening, to Exeter, with nothing, during the whole journey, to disturb his placidity beyond a sudden rainstorm; and that didn't disturb it. Some people are natural travellers; others are not. Thoresby, who was always travelling, was a bad traveller; so were Swift and Gray and Walpole. Gay, who was happily named, was a good traveller and would no doubt have found nothing very inconvenient about even the roads of Lancashire or Sussex. Had he been ditched, fat and indolent as he was, he would probably have made himself as comfortable as possible, and have waited blandly for somebody to come along and un-ditch him. In coaches, fat men were not popular—Johnson, himself fat, remarked how many friendships had been jolted to death in a coach—but generally, the fat men, like Gay, made better travelling companions than the lean, who were apt to be easily irritated.

Swift's fretfulness and impatience as a traveller are seen in the diary he kept at Holyhead while waiting five days for a boat. Nothing was right; even the journey from Chester was full of those pricks which the fretful always attract. The guide was a knave. Swift's servant's horse lost his two fore-shoes. His own horse lost a fore-shoe. He and his servant walked three miles over a rocky road to an ale-house where there was no ale. He took the ferry to Holyhead, and dined at the inn on a loin of mutton, the worst ale in the world, and no wine. Next day he had for dinner "a raw chicken" and brandy and water. In the evening a packet-boat arrived with some "Irish claret." He secured a bottle, "which was bad enough." He had to wear a shirt for three days. The following day he dined on another loin of mutton, "so tough I could not chew it."

It rained all night and all the next day. The master of the boat that was waiting for fair weather "hath not treated me with the least civility." He went for a walk and was overtaken by a furious shower. The chimney of his room smoked. He found a dog better company than the Vicar, though "you may know a Welsh dog as well as a Welsh man or woman, by its peevish passionate way of barking." After seven days' wait, resignation came to him: "I have not spirit enough now left me to fret." He had none of the spirit of a traveller of the preceding century, who could write in *his* diary: "Up, finding our beds good, but lousy, which made us merry."

Travel certainly was trying to the temper, and still is, but the sensible man accepts the trial. Thomas Pennant, writing later in the century, looked back to his youth in 1739, and its ways of travel. Single men, he said, wearing jack-boots and trousers up to their middle, rode post through thick and thin, and, "guarded against the mire, defying the frequent stumble and fall, arose and pursued their journey with alacrity; while in these days their enervated posterity sleep away their rapid journeys in easy chaises." Describing a coach journey from Chester to London in that year, he says:

> The first day, with much labour, we got from Chester to Whitchurch, 20 miles; the second day to the Welsh Harp; the third, to Coventry; the fourth, to Northampton; the fifth, to Dunstable; and, as a wondrous effort, on the last to London before the commencement of night. The strain and labour of six good horses, sometimes eight, drew us through the sloughs of Meriden and other places. We were constantly out two hours before day, and as late at night; and in the depth of winter proportionably later.

At about that time a mighty traveller was going to and fro along the English roads, not to look about him for the "remarkable and curious," but to carry instruction and illumination to those in darkness. A mighty traveller he was, since he often did, on horseback and on bogged or broken roads, sixty miles in a day. Even at the age of eighty-eight, in the year before he died, he was still travelling, though by chaise instead of horseback, to Norwich, Lincoln, Bath, etc. Any one of his journeys would have given Swift a long fit of the spleen, but John Wesley did them as something to be done. He mentions the mishaps and the snowstorms and gales, and the fatigue, but he only mentions them; there is no peevishness.

His *Journal* is mainly a record of his ministrations and his work for the faith, but he does not disdain to set down minor detail about his travels and the roads and the weather. In one passage he mentions that in seven months he had travelled, on horseback, 2,400 miles. He rode in rain, frost, snow, and gale, and seems to have been as tough as a waggoner:

> The wind was turned full north, and blew so exceeding hard and keen that when we came to Hatfield, neither my companions nor I had much use of our hands and feet. After resting an hour, we bore up again through the wind and snow, which drove full in our faces. But this was only a squall. In Baldock field the storm began in earnest. The large hail drove so vehemently in our faces that we could not see nor hardly breathe. . . . After a short bait at Bugden we pushed on and were met in the middle of an open field with so violent a storm of rain and hail as we had not had before. It drove through our coats, great and small, boots, and everything, and yet froze as it fell, even upon our eyebrows, so that we had scarce either strength or motion left when we came into our inn at Stilton.

And after a journey of that kind, he would, directly he had reached his destination, hold a meeting and preach the Word. The storm continued next day, but he went on:

> We took the advantage of a fair blast to set out, and made the best of our way to Stamford heath. But here a new difficulty arose, from the

snow lying in large drifts. Sometimes horse and man were well-nigh swallowed up. Yet in less than an hour we were brought safe to Stamford.

Next morning his servant came to him and told him there could be no travelling that day: so much snow had fallen in the night that the roads were quite blocked up. But that could not stop John Wesley. If they couldn't ride, they could walk, and lead their horses, and should be able to do twenty miles in a day. "So in the name of God we set out. The north-east wind was piercing as a sword, and had driven the snow into such uneven heaps, that the main road was unpassable. However, we kept on, afoot or on horseback, till we came to the White Lion at Grantham."

Another time, when he was fifty-five, he had as bad a journey; ninety miles in frost, flood, and gale:

> I set out in a post-chaise between four and five in the morning; but the frost made it so bad driving that my companion came with the lame horses into Stamford as soon as me. The next stage I went on horseback: but I was then obliged to leave my mare, and take another post-chaise. I came to Bawtry about six . . . I knew no chaise could go the rest of the road; so it remained only to hire horses and a guide.
>
> We set out about seven, but I soon found my guide knew no more of the way than myself. However, we got pretty well to Idlestop about four miles from Bawtry, where we had just light to discern the river at our side and the country covered with water. I had heard that one Richard Wright lived thereabouts who knew the road over the moor perfectly well. Hearing one speak (for we could not see him), I called, "Who is there?" He answered, "Richard Wright." I soon agreed with him, and he quickly mounted his horse and rode boldly forward. The north-east wind blew full in our face: and I heard them say, "It is very cold!" But neither my face, nor hands, nor feet were cold, till between nine and ten we came to Epworth; after travelling more than ninety miles, I was little more tired that when I rose in the morning.

With all his travelling he yet contrived to keep up his reading. When he was not riding, he had other occupations, so his only time for reading was the hours spent on horseback. Riding with the reins loose on the horse's neck, he found that the horse could make its way perfectly without stumbling, and that he could give his eyes and attention to his book. It sounds incredible that a man could read close type on a jogging horse on those pitted roads, but Wesley did it as he did other incredible things.

To be benighted in those times, on a moonless night and without a lantern, was a prospect that filled timid travellers with panic. On the highway, the situation was not too dangerous, but in byways where the road was not clearly a road but a mere track, travellers were often afraid to move. Fielding mentions this panic in *Tom Jones*, when Jones and Partridge, having hired a guide to take them to Coventry, find that he does not know the way. After riding six miles from their inn, they find themselves no nearer the lights of Coventry, but stuck in a dirty lane:

> Jones now declared that they must certainly have lost their way; but this the guide insisted upon was impossible; a word which, in common conversation, is often used to signify not only improbable, but often what is really likely, and sometimes, what hath certainly happened. . . . It is not, perhaps, easy for a reader who hath never been in those circumstances to imagine the horror with which darkness, rain and wind fill persons who have lost their way in the night and who consequently have not the pleasant prospect of warm fires, dry clothes, and other refreshments to support their minds in struggling with the inclemencies of the weather. A very imperfect idea of this horror will, however, serve sufficiently to account for the conceits which now filled the head of Partridge. . . .

When a traveller was indeed benighted and out of his road, any light was a beacon, and it was almost the right of any decent traveller to approach the house and request shelter. More than once, Jones and Partridge, when benighted on their journeys, made for any light that they saw, and sought, and usually received, the hospitality of the house, or, in one case, of a gipsy encampment. Sometimes they were not so lucky. Outside Gloucester one night, when they had missed their way, Partridge saw a light, and at once concluded that their troubles were at an end. But when they arrived at the house, their first knock received no answer. After hammering for some time, an upper window was opened, and an old woman asked what they wanted. Jones explained that they had lost their way, and having seen a light in the window were seeking shelter. The woman refused to admit them. Partridge begged that they might be admitted for a few minutes, to warm themselves by the fire, since they were almost dead with the cold:

> He assured her that the gentleman who spoke to her was one of the greatest squires in the country; and made use of every argument, save one, which Jones afterwards effectually added; and this was, the promise of half-a-crown—a bribe too great to be resisted by such a person, especially as the genteel appearance of Jones, which the light of the moon plainly discovered to her, together with his affable behaviour, had entirely subdued those apprehensions of thieves which she had at first conceived. She agreed therefore, at last, to let them in; where Partridge, to his infinite joy, found a good fire ready for his reception.

The inns made sharp distinctions between foot travellers, waggon travellers, public coach travellers, and those riding their own horses or travelling in their own coaches. Some inns took nobody but "quality"; that is, the two last-named classes. Those inns that received stage-coach travellers seldom took waggon company or foot travellers; the hedge inn was considered good enough for them. When they did take them, they set them to dine in the kitchen with the coachmen and postillions and servants of the "quality." Though sometimes the upper servants of the "quality" strongly objected to sit down with foot travellers or waggon-folk. Fielding shows Sophia's maid lamenting that, though they were staying only a short time, she had not ordered a private room for herself, and refusing to sup off a joint of cold roast beef which had been in general use at the table. She entreated the landlady not to make her sick, and protested that if she had fasted a month she could not eat what had been touched by such fellows. She then ordered eggs and bacon, and:

> While the supper was preparing, Mrs. Abigail began to lament she had not ordered a fire in the parlour; but, she said, that was now too late. "However," said she, "I have novelty to recommend a kitchen; for I do not believe I ever eat in one before." Then, turning to the post-boys, she asked them Why they were not in the stable with their horses. "If I must eat my hard fare here, madam," cries she to the landlady, "I beg the kitchen may be kept clear, that I may not be surrounded with all the blackguards in town; as for you, sir," says she to Partridge, "you look somewhat like a gentleman, and may sit still if you please; I don't desire to disturb anybody but mob."

In the same novel, the landlady of an inn, after giving rough words to an ill-dressed woman who arrives on foot with Tom Jones, discovers that she is "quality," and at once begins to grovel and ask pardon for her offences. She begged "that all might be imputed to ignorance of her quality; for Lud, madam, says she, how should I have imagined that a lady of your fashion would appear in such a dress? I am sure, madam, if I had once suspected that your ladyship was your ladyship, I would sooner have burned my tongue out than have said what I have said."

The contemptuous attitude to waggon-folk is reflected in a scene in Smollett. Roderick Random and Strap, journeying to London by waggon, one day reached an inn where the waggon ordinarily dined, and found that the dinner intended for the waggon company had been claimed by some earlier arrivals. But the waggoner, a man of spirit, stood up for his rights and the rights of his passengers:

On the sixth day, while we were about to sit down to dinner, the inn-keeper came and told us that three gentlemen, just arrived, had ordered the victuals to be carried to their apartment, although he had informed them that they were bespoke by the passengers in the waggon. To which information they had replied, "The passengers in the waggon might be damned—their betters must be served before them—they supposed it would be no hardship on such travellers to dine upon bread and cheese for one day." This was a terrible disappointment to us all; and we laid our heads together how to remedy it; when Miss Jenny observed that Captain Weazel, being by profession a soldier, ought in this case to protect and prevent us from being insulted. But the captain excused himself, saying he would not for all the world be known to have travelled in a waggon; swearing at the same time that, could he appear with honour, they should eat his sword sooner than his provision. Upon this declaration, Miss Jenny, snatching his weapon, drew it and ran immediately into the kitchen, where she threatened to put the cook to death if he did not send the victuals into our chamber immediately. The noise she made brought the three strangers down, one of whom no sooner perceived her than he cried, "Ha! Jenny Ramper! what the devil brought thee hither?" "My dear Jack Rattle!" replied she, running into his arms, "is it you? Then Weazel may go to hell for a dinner—I shall dine with you." They con-sented to this proposal with a great deal of joy; and we were on the point of being reduced to a very uncomfortable meal, when Joey, understanding the whole affair, entered the kitchen with a pitchfork in his hand, and swore he would be the death of any man who should pretend to seize the victuals prepared for the waggon. This menace had like to have produced fatal consequences; the three strangers drawing their swords, and being joined by their servants, and we ranging ourselves on the side of Joey; when the landlord, interposing, offered to part with his own dinner to keep the peace, which was accepted by the strangers; and we sat down at table without further molestation.

The simple Parson Adams, when travelling with Joseph Andrews and Fanny, was usually shown to the kitchen; no particular respect was paid to the "cloth" unless its pockets held money. When he had a horse, he and Joseph travelled by a method of the time called Ride and Tie. The two set out together, one on horseback and one on foot. When the one on horseback had covered a certain number of miles, he dismounted, tied the horse to a tree or gate, and went forward on foot. The other, on reaching the place where the horse was tethered, mounted and galloped past his friend, until he had had his share of riding, when he in turn dismounted and left the horse for the friend to pick up; and so on.

A pleasing custom of that time, unhappily abandoned long ago, was that by which on Sundays, when respectable travellers broke

their journeys, the landlords of the better sort of inns made those
under their roof on that day literally their guests. The invitation,
Scott says, was usually complied with by all whose distinguished rank
did not induce them to think compliance a derogation. He shows
one of his heroes, Frank Osbaldistone, during some weeks' journey,
accepting each Sabbath the hospitality of the host of his inn:

> The honest publican, dilated into additional consequence by a sense
> of his own importance, while presiding among the guests on whom it was
> his ordinary duty to attend, was in himself an entertaining spectacle; and
> around his genial orbit, other planets of inferior consequence performed
> their revolutions. The wits and humorists, the distinguished worthies of
> the town or village, the apothecary, the attorney, even the curate himself,
> did not disdain to partake of this hebdomadal festivity. The guests
> assembled from different quarters, and following different professions,
> formed, in language, manners and sentiments, a curious contrast to each
> other, not indifferent to those who desired to possess a knowledge of
> mankind in its varieties.

The practice which to-day is called hitch-hiking was commonly
used at that time. Charlotte Clarke, Colley Cibber's daughter, as
a strolling player, got about the country by all manner of means.
She usually wore men's dress and was often accepted as a man.
Sometimes she and a fellow-player hired a "double horse" (pillion),
sometimes they were given a lift in a hay-cart going their way, and
sometimes they had threepennyworth of waggon. On one occasion,
she and a friend, being penniless, sold a few of their things for four
shillings, and went on foot from Devizes to Romsey. The road across
Salisbury Plain was forty miles, but as there were no houses on that
road for travellers, they had to go round, through the villages, which
added a further twenty miles. Their night's expenses at Devizes, for
lodging and supper came to ninepence (they must have lodged at
a drover's ale-house) and they set out to do the sixty miles with three
shillings and threepence between them:

> After a most deplorable, half-starving journey, through intricate roads
> and terrible showers of rain, in three days' time we arrived at Romsey,
> having parted from our last three half-pence to ride five miles in a waggon,
> to the great relief of our o'er-tired legs. It may be scarce believed that
> two people should travel so far upon so small a pittance, who had not
> been from their birth enured to hardships; but we positively did, and, in
> the extream heat of the day, were often glad to have recourse to a clear
> stream to quench our thirst after a tedious, painful march; not only to
> save our money, but enable us to go through the toil of the day till the
> friendly inn received us.

34　A Village Alehouse of the Eighteenth Century

35　A Country Inn
From an engraving of 1791

36   A Carrier's Cart outside a Country Inn
From a print of ca. 1800

37   A Stage-Wagon of *ca.* 1805
From an engraving by Pyne

Even rank and money could not always ensure a comfortable journey or an inn for the night. Horace Walpole, on some of his little tours, was landed more than once in what he called "piteous distresses," but he seems to have accepted them with his usual arid equanimity. At Tonbridge his inn was full of farmers and tobacco; and next morning, when he wanted to see Penshurst, he could not go: the only man in the town who had two horses would not let them out because the bad roads might damage them. He sent to Tunbridge Wells for others, and had to wait half the day for them. After Lamberhurst, "the roads grew bad beyond all badness, the night dark beyond all darkness, and our guide frightened beyond all frightfulness." He somehow got up (or down, he wasn't sure which) a famous precipice called Silver Hill and at ten o'clock arrived at "a wretched village." At the inn only one bed was to be had; the rest were taken by smugglers. So, with links and lanterns, he went on. At two o'clock in the morning he got to a worse village, with a worse inn crammed with excise officers, but managed to secure beds. The tour ended with an abortive visit to Hever ("we could not find our way and were forced to return, and again lost ourselves in coming from Penshurst") and a visit to Lord Westmorland's seat at Mereworth, where the hospitality of the house made his postillion so drunk that he overturned the chaise on the bank of a river, and just missed the river itself.

On another tour he found at Wellingborough what he called the beastliest inn upon earth, where he was given a vast bed-chamber which he took to be the club-room, since it stunk of tobacco. Travelling down to Peterborough, he wanted to go to Ely, and was directed to go by way of Huntingdon, since rain and floods made the direct way impassable. From Huntingdon he was sent south to Cambridge, still on his way north to Ely, but had to abandon the Ely visit on reports of inundations and narrow escapes. Reporting another tour, he has an odd note on Birmingham; at least, odd for us of to-day: "Birmingham is large, and swarms with people and trade, but did not answer my expectation from any *beauty* in it."

During the last days of March 1750, the roads out of London afforded an interesting spectacle. They were thronged with a traffic of coach, horse, and foot in a great exodus. It was the first flight since that of the Plague year, 1665, but it was not caused by plague or fire or threatened invasion. It was caused by some Bedlamite prophet who had foretold an approaching earthquake which was to engulf all London. Walpole, in a letter to Montagu, gave an account of it:

H

I told you the women talked of going out of town: several families are literally gone, and many more going to-day and to-morrow; for what adds to the absurdity is that the second shock having happened exactly a month after the former, it prevails that there will be a third on Thursday next, another month, which is to swallow up London.

In a following letter he gives further details, from which we may see that Siren Suits are nothing very new:

I return to the earthquake, which I had mistaken: it is to be to-day. This frantic terror prevails so much that within these three days seven-hundred-and-thirty coaches have been counted passing Hyde Park corner with whole parties removing into the country. Here is a good advertisement which I cut out of the paper to-day—"On Monday next will be published (price 6*d*.) a true and exact list of all the Nobility and Gentry who have left, or shall leave, this place through fear of another earthquake."
Several women have made earthquake gowns: that is, warm gowns to sit out of doors all night. These are of the more courageous. One woman, still more heroic, is come to town on purpose; she says all her friends are in London, and she will not survive them. But what will you think of Lady Catherine Pelham, Lady Frances Arundel, and Lord and Lady Galway, who go this evening to an inn ten miles out of town, where they are to play at brag till five in the morning, and then come back—I suppose to look for the bones of their husbands and families under the rubbish.

One of the oddest travel narratives of that time was written by Jonas Hanway—merchant, philanthropist, hater of tea-drinking, and the first man to walk abroad with an umbrella. *Eight Days' Journey from Portsmouth to Kingston on Thames, with Miscellaneous Thoughts* (1755) is a record, in letter form, of a journey made with Two Ladies. It was this book that led Johnson to remark that Hanway made some reputation by travelling abroad, and lost it all by travelling at home. The oddity, apart from the style, is that the letters are addressed to the Two Ladies who accompanied him, so that he is giving an account of the journey to those who made it, and describing places and incidents which they had themselves seen and shared. The journey itself was as odd as the account of it.

Hanway was a good deal of an old maid, sententious and ponderous, and much given to "thoughts." The journey has much the air of a journey made by three female Sunday-school teachers. On the road they discussed Death, the Immortality of the Soul, the Nature of God, the Vanity of Life, Virtue, Matrimony, Temperance, Resignation, Charity, and—the Advantages of Female Conversation, of which, even after eight days of it, he seems not to have had enough. Setting out from Salisbury, one of the company "beguiled the way with interesting and affecting stories of departed friends, how entirely they were reconciled to death." Their inn at Widgate "was not of the most elegant kind, but such is our happiness in this fertile island, we are ever secure against the terrors of hunger though we cannot always enjoy a luxurious superfluity." After Widgate, they travelled over "delicious downs," and "the gay morn glittered with dewy gems." But at Blandford they found the town filled with soldiers, and none of the party seems to have had much military enthusiasm. The month was August, the time of manœuvres and reviews, and for the rest of their journey they were haunted by soldiers. The inns were crowded with them, and when they did find rooms they had little sleep because of the noise made, they thought, "by a thousand giants mounted on elephants." Wyley was "but a mean village, and lies on low ground." He mentions that they had to walk to the inn on the causeway, since the road leading to it was full of water. After dining, they set out for Amesbury, over Salisbury Plain, and he mentions the absence of the lately introduced mile-stones. "The computed miles of these cross-roads appear much longer than measured ones; or perhaps it is because here are no milestones which, by convincing us that we are in the right path, beguile the way."

Their reception at Amesbury was "inconvenient." More soldiers. The hostess assured them that she had ample accommodation, and led them to an apartment containing fifteen to twenty soldiers. Mr. Hanway at once conducted the ladies to another house, "not without a sensibility of that pleasure which true gallantry always affords to minds not devoid of generosity." On the way from Ames-bury to Stockbridge, he was so moved by the beauty of the country that he headed the letter describing that stage—A Rhapsody:

> The zephyrs which now sported in the air, the brightness of the sky, and the beautiful variety and verdure of the earth seemed to vie with each other whether they should most enchant the mind with the love of rural joys or excite a contempt of those pleasures that nourish the corroding passions which prevail in great cities. It was in this morning's journey that my imagination took a distant flight above the earth. The brightness of the azure sky received an uncommon beauty from the clouds which flew on high, clothed in milky white, and presented to the eye of my fancy the appearance of an *angel*. . . .

Except for the inconvenience of finding every town filled with soldiers, the eight days' journey was accomplished with only one disturbing incident. That, perhaps, was a just visitation. At Stock-bridge, he and the Two Ladies, after all their moral disquisitions, went to the races, and on coming away:

How near was your post-chaise from being tumbled over by a coach-wheel! An ounce of weight more had done it. I was sorry to observe that some who *ride* in coaches have as little politeness as those who *drive* them; if this were not the case, the gentleman who saw the accident would have asked your pardon. What dangers surround us in the common occurrences of life! Our pursuits of the most innocent amusements are not exempt from them.

The journey continued through Farnham, Guildford, and Epsom, and ended at Kingston, where he parted from his female companions on a high valedictory note:

The magic wand which had given objects so many charms was broken: the happiness which I had fondly ascribed to my own disposition to be pleased, I discovered was owing to my companions' power of pleasing. Life itself has an end: we must rise from a banquet with gratitude for the pleasure we have received . . . and though I am now reduced to a level with common mortals, to find my way about the world in the best manner I can . . .

And so on. It is far from the true sadness and the sonorous cadence of Fitzgerald's Farewell dedication to *Salaman and Absal*, but it must have given a fluttering to the Two Ladies.

Many new methods of road-making were tried during the latter half of the century, none of them meeting very well the demands of heavier and increasing traffic. One of the most remarkable road-makers of the time was John Metcalf, called Blind Jack of Knaresborough. He was born blind, yet he had a most varied life. He acted as a guide across the moors on which he had been brought up. He once walked from London to York, knowing nothing of that road. During the '45, he marched with a regiment from Yorkshire into Scotland. He was also a chapman, a fiddler, a carrier, and eventually a road-maker. He constructed, or re-made, some two hundred miles of road; but his work was confined to Yorkshire and Lancashire, and the roads of the south received no benefit from his ideas and methods. Hence the frequent outbursts of Arthur Young.

Arthur Young, the agriculturist, made Rural Rides some fifty years before Cobbett, and in the *Six Weeks' Tour through the Southern Counties* (1768) he has much to say about roads, and says it as lustily as Cobbett said his things about paper money and the National Debt. Writing from Essex, he lets out thus:

Of all the cursed roads that ever disgraced this kingdom in the very ages of barbarism, none ever equalled that from Billericay to the King's Head at Tilbury. It is for near twelve miles so narrow that a mouse cannot pass

38   Packhorses loaded with Yorkshire Cloth

39   Stonebreakers working on a Road
Both from engravings by George Walker, 1814

40 Travellers taking refreshment at a Country Alehouse, while
a Stage-Wagon rumbles by

From a print of ca. 1800

41 Unloading a Wagon

From a print by Rowlandson

by any carriage; I saw a fellow creep under his waggon to assist me to lift, if possible, my chaise over a hedge. The ruts are of an incredible depth— and a pavement of diamonds might as well be sought for as a quarter. The trees everywhere overgrow the road, so that it is totally impervious to the sun except at a few places. And to add to all the infamous circumstances which concur to plague a traveller, I must not forget the eternally meeting with chalk-waggons, themselves frequently stuck fast till a collection of them are in the same situation, and twenty or thirty horses may be tacked to each to draw them out one by one.

And again:

The country from Tetford to Oxford is extremely disagreeable, barren, wild and almost uninhabited. The road called, by a vile prostitution of language, a turnpike, but christened, I apprehend, by people who know not what a road is; it is all of chalkstone, of which loose ones are everywhere roaming about to lame horses. It is full of holes, and the ruts very deep; and withal so narrow that I with great difficulty got my chair out of the way of the Witney waggons and various machines which are perpetually passing. The tolls are very dear and vilely unreasonable, considering the badness of the roads.

And yet again:

The road from Witney to Northleach is, I think, the worst turnpike I ever travelled in; so bad that it is a scandal to the country. They mend and make with nothing but the stone which forms the under stratum all over the country. . . . This stone, which rises in vast flakes, would make an admirable foundation for a surface of gravel; but by using it alone, and in pieces as large as one's head, the road is rendered most execrable. I travelled it with a very low opinion of all the counties and places it leads to: for if they were inhabited by people of fortune and spirit, I should think they would never suffer such a barbarous method of mending their capital road to subsist.

At the end of his book he mentions that all travellers should have some knowledge of the inns on the road on which they are travelling. The want of that knowledge may land them in some disagreeable places. In the hope, therefore, of helping others, he gives a list of the inns he stopped at during his tour, with his comments on the inns themselves, the manners of the servants, and the charges. Some of his comments are as outspoken as his comments on the roads they could not be made by a modern writer on any inn of to-day without bringing a writ.

Of an inn at Northleach, he notes: "Very bad and very dear." Of one inn at Cardiff, he says only "Bad"; and of another in the same place "Worse." Of an inn at Wanstead: "Dirty and dear." Of his

H*

Winchester inn: "Impertinent and dirty." Some of his favourable comments may have caused jealousy between certain inns; as when he says of an inn at Holkham: "Clean, civil, and reasonable"; and of the Duke's Head at King's Lynn: "*Exceeding* civil and very reasonable." And of an inn at Oxford: "Good"; and at High Wycombe: "Exceeding good, civil and not unreasonable." His comment on the Bear, at Devizes, is not unexpected by those who know their social history: "Exceedingly good and remarkably civil." Naturally; it was kept at that time by the father of the future Sir Thomas Lawrence, P.R.A. Fanny Burney described the mother as a hostess with whom she was much pleased, and who "seemed something above her station." All the family, she added, were "strikingly handsome."

Innkeeping at that time was a serious calling, and innkeepers had a rather higher standing than men engaged in trade. Many of them were men of substance and position in their towns. Defoe, earlier in the century, described the landlord of his inn at Doncaster: "He was mayor of the town as well as post-master; kept a pack of hounds, and was company for the best gentlemen in the neighbourhood." Some of them were councillors, one was a magistrate, and in almost all towns they were among the leading men.

Johnson's appreciation of good inns is everybody's knowledge: it was at "an excellent inn at Chapel House," near Chipping Norton, when he and Boswell were on their Midland tour, that he delivered that much-quoted eulogy of inns. But he was also a critic, and a casual reference in Boswell may not be so well known. It makes one wish that we had a few Johnsons with us to stir up some of our modern innkeepers:

> At the inn where we stopped he was exceedingly dissatisfied with some roast mutton which he had for dinner. . . . He scolded the waiter, saying, "It is as bad as bad can be: it is ill-fed, ill-killed, ill-kept, and ill-dressed."

He also appreciated travel, as a man must needs do to set out in those days, at the age of sixty-five, on that tour of the Western Islands. His travelling was done by both stage-coach and private post-chaise. He was an agreeable fellow passenger to the company of any stage-coach, but he preferred the speed of the post-chaise. As he said to Boswell when they were whirling in a post-chaise through the Midlands—"Life has not many things better than this." Stage-coach travel had an etiquette of its own. There was a certain unwritten code of manners to be observed, such as avoiding disputes and dining together. When Roderick Random travelled to Bath, a good deal of incivility and hat-cocking passed, and when, at the inn where the coach dined, two couples engaged separate rooms and dined in private, a lawyer was moved to remark that he had been a traveller for twenty years, and never knew the stage-coach rules so much infringed before. As each driver of a coach completed his stage, he expected a tip. There was a sort of fixed tariff on the different roads, and when Boswell on one occasion gave the driver a shilling, Johnson, who knew the etiquette, as he knew everything else (did he ever say "Sir, I don't know"?) took Boswell aside and scolded him. He pointed out that the custom was for each passenger to give sixpence, and what Boswell had done would make the coachman dissatisfied with the rest of the passengers.

At about that time guards were introduced, armed with blunderbuss and sword. In the early days there had been no guard, but the driver was furnished with blunderbuss or musket, and powder and shot, which he kept under the box-seat. Most advertisements of coaches of the later years mentioned their guards, as being men of civil manners and "fully armed." About 1780 certain coaches were put on the road which broke the old-time rule of halting for the night. They ran right through, pausing only for supper and breakfast, and the necessary changes of horses. In 1784, as Charles Harper tells us in his *Stage Coach and Mail*, the first royal mail-coach was put on the road by a coaching company of Bath. It did the journey to or from London in sixteen hours, and thus introduced the new era of speed. But it was not until the last days of coaching—1820-30— that speed rather than safety became an essential consideration. Mail-coaches then achieved, on flat roads, twelve miles an hour, with change of horses at every seven miles.

But through the latter years of the eighteenth century the speed for the mail-coach remained at about six miles per hour, and for the stage-coach about five, or on bad roads four. The waggon still did about two, and seems never to have done much better even in its last days on the improved roads of the middle nineteenth century.

Some very vivid pictures of English travel towards the end of the century are those presented in the travel letters of the German pastor, Carl Philipp Moritz, who visited England and went about it in 1782. He was acutely observant, and his letters are full of that Dutch detail which brings a scene right to our eyes in breathing life. Take his description of a post-chaise and its postillion when he rode from Dartford to London:

> These carriages are very neat and lightly built, so that you hardly perceive their motion as they roll along these firm smooth roads; they have windows in front and on both sides. The horses are generally good,

and the postillions particularly smart and active, and always ride on a full trot. The one we had wore his hair cut short, a round hat, and a brown jacket of tolerable fine cloth, with a nosegay in his bosom. Now and then, when he drove very hard, he looked round and with a smile seemed to solicit our approbation.

Anxious to see men and manners at close quarters, he made his travels mainly on foot, not knowing, when he set out, how foot travellers were regarded in England. He soon learned. He found himself either refused or shown into the kitchen among the boors. He was addressed by the casual term of "Master" in place of the usual "Sir" given to coach passengers. Sometimes, when asking for a room, he had the door slammed in his face. Once, having been granted a bed, he was told later that he could not have it; they had discovered that he was travelling on foot. At another place he heard himself spoken of as "a poor travelling creature" in tones which rang in his ears as expressing all the English contempt for outcast wretches without house or home. When he did secure a bed, landlords, waiters, and chambermaids either ignored him or treated him with scorn. In Germany, apparently, at that time, a decent man could travel on foot without attracting remark. The fact that he was saving his money by a cheap mode of travel did not expose him to obloquy, but in England:

> A traveller on foot in this country seems to be considered as a sort of wild man, or an out-of-the-way being, who is stared at, pitied, suspected, and shunned by everybody that meets him.

And again:

> I was now confirmed in my suspicions that, in England, any person undertaking so long a journey on foot is sure to be looked upon and con- sidered as either a beggar or a vagabond, or some necessitous wretch, which is a character not much more popular than that of a rogue. . . But with all my partiality for this country, it is impossible, even in theory, and much less so in practice, to approve of a system which confines all the pleasures and benefits of travel to the rich. A poor peripatetic is hardly allowed even the humble merit of being honest.

But he went on his way with a cheerful mind, prepared to please and to be pleased. His picture of the inn kitchen at Nettlebed, near Henley, is an excellent interior:

> The chimney in this kitchen, where they were roasting and boiling, seemed to be taken off from the rest of the room and enclosed by a wooden partition: the rest of the apartment was made use of as a sitting and eating room. All round on the sides were shelves with pewter dishes and plates,

800

42   A Post-chaise "scorching" through Glastonbury, Somerset

From a drawing of ca. 1800

43 A Post-chaise, leaving Oxford, halted at the Turnpike on the London Road

From a drawing of ca. 1800

44 A Post-chaise outside the "White Hart" at Reigate

From an aquatint by Rowlandson and Wigstead of 1790

and the ceiling was well stored with provisions of various kinds, such as sugar-loaves, black-puddings, hams, sausages, flitches of bacon, etc.

Excellent, too, is his description of the all-night orgy at the Mitre, Oxford, with the clergymen of Oxford, all in their gowns and bands, all drinking pots of strong ale, and banging the table in theological argument. The party broke up at dawn, when one of the Reverends exclaimed: "Damme, I must read prayers this morning at All Souls'!" As Moritz had been so well introduced he was allowed, though a foot traveller, to have a bed at the Mitre; but was ashamed to own that when he awoke he "had got so dreadful an headache from the copious and numerous toasts of my jolly and reverend friends that I could not possibly get up."

At Sutton, near Birmingham, he found a lodging at a simple ale-house, and was shown into the kitchen, where he met something of a curiosity. "The company consisted of a female chimney-sweeper and her children who . . . soon drank to my health and began a conversation with me." The lady chimney-sweeper had a romantic story, and he learned that she and her husband were worth a thousand pounds, not counting their plate and furniture. At another inn, near Derby, he found another character in the landlord. The landlord, on learning that he was a German, took it for granted that he could play the French horn. When Moritz asked why he assumed this, the landlord explained that when he was a boy a German had stopped at their inn, and had played the French horn very well.

Having learned an unpleasant lesson by travelling on foot, he made one or two other journeys by coach. But he still tried to do the thing cheaply, and again found himself in trouble. He describes the coaches as quite elegant, lined in the inside, and with two seats large enough to accommodate six persons, though the company, when the coach was full, was rather crowded. On his first journey, as an inside passenger, he noted that the English had a curious habit of riding on the roof of a coach, a mode first introduced in 1753. Those to whom it was not convenient to pay the full price could, for a lower price, sit on the top of the coach, but without any seats or even a rail. He did not at that time discover how they travelled without falling off, but on a later journey he travelled in that way himself. Outside passengers could also, if they chose, ride in the luggage basket, or rumble, which was half-filled with straw. After trying both modes of outside riding he came to the conclusion—Never Again:

This ride from Leicester to Northampton I shall remember as long as I live. . . . My companions on the top of the coach were a farmer, a young

man very decently dressed, and a blackamoor. The getting up alone
was at the risk of one's life; and when I was up I was obliged to sit just at
the corner of the coach, with nothing to hold by but a sort of little handle,
fastened on the side. I sat nearest the wheel; and the moment that we
set off I fancied that I saw certain death await me. . . . The machine
now rolled along with prodigious rapidity, over the stones through the
town, and every moment we seemed to fly into the air; so that it was
almost a miracle that we still stuck to the coach and did not fall. . . .
At last, the being continually in fear of my life became insupportable, and
as we were going up a hill, and consequently proceeding rather slower than
usual, I crept from the top of the coach and got snug into the basket.

"O sir, sir, you will be shaken to death!" said the black. As long as we
went up hill, it was easy and pleasant . . . but how was the case altered
when we came to go down hill; then all the trunks and parcels began, as
it were, to dance around me, and every thing in the basket seemed to be
alive; and I every moment received from them such violent blows that I
thought my last hour was come. . . . I was obliged to suffer the torture
nearly an hour till we came to another hill again, when quite shaken to
pieces and sadly bruised I again crept to the top of the coach. . . . I
now write this as a warning to all strangers to stage-coaches who may
happen to take it into their heads, without being used to it, to take a
place on the outside of an English post-coach; and still more, a place in the
basket.

Moritz, as his picture shows, was a hardy fellow and a spirited
traveller, able to survive all the woes and inflictions that the road
might offer. But at that time of increasing facilities for travel there
were many good folk whom nothing could tempt to the road, and
who spent their lives without going more than ten miles from their
home. Travel to them implied all that it implied to the people of
the fourteenth century. There were others, equally timid, who did
occasionally screw themselves up to making a journey, but however
short it might be, it involved weeks of preparation and thought; and
when they did at last set off, they first commended themselves to
heavenly protection. Cowper, the hypochondriac, who was, in any
matter outside his routine, as timid as the hares he kept as pets, made
quite an epic of the one journey he was induced to make—from
Buckinghamshire to Sussex, to visit William Hayley, the patron of
William Blake and many others.

All his correspondents heard about it; first as a project, then as a
possibility, then as a settled decision, and finally as achieved. But
while it was a project his letters are full of tremors concerning it.
He speaks of a thousand lions, monsters and giants being in the way,
but thinks they may vanish if he has the courage to face them.

Writing to the Rev. William Bull, he speaks of having sat for his picture, and goes on to say that that is not the only prodigy he has to tell of:

> A greater belongs to me; and one that you will hardly credit, even on my own testimony. We are on the eve of a journey, and a long one. On this very day se'nnight we set out for Eartham, the seat of my brother bard, Mr. Hayley, on the other side of London, nobody knows where, a hundred and twenty miles off. Pray for us, my friend, that we may have a safe going and return. It is a tremendous exploit, and I feel a thousand anxieties when I think of it.

Writing to Hayley himself about it, he says that if Hayley had any conception of the fears he has had to battle with, he would wonder that he still persevered in his resolution to undertake it. But as the day drew nearer, the terrors began to abate, and he had the example of Mrs. Unwin, an invalid, who looked forward to the journey quite calmly. When, at last, the journey was accomplished, he writes in high spirits:

> This journey . . . has by the mercy of God been happily and well performed, and we have met with no terrors by the way. I indeed myself was a little daunted by the tremendous height of the Sussex hills, in comparison of which all that I had seen elsewhere are dwarfs; but I only was alarmed; Mrs. Unwin had no such sensations, but was always cheerful from the beginning of our expedition to the end of it. At Barnet we found the inn so noisy that I was almost driven to despair by the dread that she would get no sleep; but I was happily disappointed. . . . At Ripley we had a silent inn, and rested well. The next day, but late, we arrived at Eartham; and now begin to feel ourselves, under the hospitable roof of our amiable friend, well requited for all the fatigue, the heat, and the clouds of dust that we endured in the journey.

To another correspondent he writes of three days' confinement in a coach, and of suffering all that could be suffered from excessive heat and dust; yet to another he says: "About myself I care little, being made of materials so tough as not to threaten me even now, at the end of so many lustrums, with anything like a speedy dissolution. My chief concern has been about Mrs. Unwin." The return journey did not, in prospect or in fact, cause any tremors:

> With no sinister accident to retard or terrify us, we find ourselves, at a quarter before one, arrived safe at Kingston. . . . That night we rested well in our inn, and at twenty minutes after eight next morning set off for London; exactly at ten we reached Mr. Rose's door; we drank a dish of chocolate with him, and proceeded, Mr. Rose riding with us as far as St.

Albans. From that time we met with no impediment. In the dark
and in a storm, at eight at night, we found ourselves at our own back door.

A narrative of English travel which is, in its bland way, amusing,
is a *Tour Through the South of England*, by Edward Daniel Clarke,
published in 1791. He went with a friend, and they took with them,
as valet, the local barber—a sort of Partridge. Travel was something new to the barber. He had never been fifty miles from his
own door, and every incident of the journey filled him with alarms.
London frightened him, and Portsmouth with its sailors bewildered
him. He had never stayed at an inn, and the hurry and confusion
of a large inn almost caused a nervous breakdown. He was always
bowing to the waiters, and stepping aside from them and colliding
with kitchen boys, and being kicked by one and pushed by the other,
so that he was constantly running to his employer for protection.

The book, for the most part, is the usual account of towns through
which the travellers passed; churches, abbeys, and scenery. But it
presents one delightful little interlude quite incongruous with a
leisurely tour of two bland bourgeois gentlemen. Somewhere in
Cornwall they were "adopted" by a sort of Jingle—an apparently
insane naval officer:

> A gentleman accosted us on landing and introduced himself to us as a
> Lieutenant in the navy. He had fastened his portmanteau behind our
> chaise, and begged permission to see it conveyed to Truro, as he under-
> stood our route lay that way. In return for this indulgence he would
> favour us with his company in the chaise, and pilot us part of our journey.
> . . . Our companion soon became sufficiently communicative; he had
> travelled over the whole globe; knew everything and everybody. Our
> company suited him of all things; we were exactly the men he liked; he
> would never quit us, and would take care we should not be imposed upon.
> . . . At Liskeard we dined; the bill displeased our pilot; he was suddenly
> enraged, and swore he would prosecute the people; stamped, cracked his
> whip, and made a great noise, when all at once, hearing the chaise was ready,
> he flew to seat himself, and left us to pay the bill. As we drove off, "Well,
> gentlemen," said he, "I see you are resolved to be cheated, and by God, I
> will never leave you till you are more acquainted with the world."

He swore at the postillion for not driving properly, and then
stopped the chaise, got out, mounted his horse, which the valet was
riding, and, saying he would no longer ride when such a scoundrel
drove, he wished them a pleasant journey, and galloped off. They
congratulated themselves on having got rid of him, but when they
arrived at Lostwithiel, there he was, all dust, without his horse,
waiting for them hat in hand, and hallooing as they approached.

When they stopped, he explained that he had secured for them a proper post-chaise with a proper postillion. They changed into the new chaise, thanked him, and drove away, leaving him there. But when they had gone about five miles, they heard a noise of galloping, and the Lieutenant came after them, riding alongside and flogging their horses, and damning the postillion:

All the way to St. Austell we were amused in this manner, and occasionally with loud quarrels between our pilot and postillion. After leaving St. Austell it grew very dark, the night became gloomy and tempestuous, and nothing was wanting to render our situation truly dismal but the prospect around us, which we were told was a wide and barren moor, rugged, black, and desolate. Suddenly the chaise stopped; our pilot presented himself at the window and demanded one of our pistols to defend himself from some highwaymen which he said he had observed. I gave him the pistol, contrary to the advice of our valet, who on his knees entreated that I would not be so imprudent. "He will shoot us and rob us, sir, as sure as you are born!" "Let him try first," said I, and taking the other pistol, I cocked it, and felt determined to fire at him the instant he attempted to interrupt us.

They went on in uncertainty for three or four miles, when suddenly the Lieutenant dashed ahead of the chaise and fired his pistol into the air. The valet collapsed into the bottom of the chaise, and the author let down the window, and asked, in God's name, what the man thought he was doing; and was answered with:

"Don't be alarmed, gentlemen! I would not for the world make you uneasy. What I did was merely for the sake of trying your pistols, and I must say they are not worth twopence." "Sir," said I, "they answer our purpose, to prevent us from interruption and to intimidate scoundrels." "And, sir," said my companion, "be kind enough to return that which you have borrowed, since you seem to have as little occasion for it as we have for your company. Sir, we wish you a good evening!" Fortunately for us, he took the hint, and we saw him no more.

By the end of the century we hear less about highwaymen. Two factors were against their trade. One—coaches were faster and not so easily stopped, and were well guarded; two—paper money, which could be traced, had come into use, so that travellers no longer had to carry bags of gold. But sometimes people were compelled to transfer real money from one part of the country to another, as when a landowner was sending his rents to a bank. On those occasions, though the danger of attack was small, all sorts of precautions were taken. Charles G. Harper, in his *Holyhead Road*, gives a description of the precautions taken by a Sir Watkin Wynne

I

of that time, when conveying his rents from North Wales to London. This was a four or five days' journey, and it was made in a bullet-proof coach, lined with iron. Four stout guards went with Sir Watkin: two on the box, with a double-barrelled gun, and two in the basket, similarly armed. Another guard sat in the coach with Sir Watkin, and two large dogs ran behind. At night, when they inned, the coach was put in the coach-house, and the dogs and two of the guards stood sentry over it until morning.

There was thus little opportunity for midnight robbers or daylight highwaymen. Few as the highwaymen were at the end of the century, they were not at any period of the Georgian age so many as they had been under the Stuarts. The most common crimes of the eighteenth century were footpad robbery and burglary from house or shop. In the whole century only three highwaymen reached an eminence that carried their names into the nineteenth— Dick Turpin, Captain Maclean, and Jack Rann; and of these only two were strictly highwaymen. Dick Turpin was mainly a deer-stealer, horse-thief, and burglar. Captain Maclean, known as the Gentleman Highwayman, was a man of decent origin, son of a clergyman. While supporting himself by working the highway, he also went fortune-hunting among the daughters of the respectable, and by his antecedents and his agreeable manners he got himself received into some quite good houses. He has only a few exploits on his record; one of them the holding-up and robbing of Horace Walpole. He seems to have been in the line of Claude du Vall, and his end evoked much female sympathy.

The most picturesque figure of the roads during that century was Jack Rann, the swaggering, audacious Sixteen-String Jack. He was first a postillion, then an officer's servant, and then private coachman. It was in this last employment that he gained his name, through his flaunting dress: his breeches had eight coloured strings at each knee. But he soon lost that respectable place and all chance of any other, and turned to the easier life of the highway. Quite early in his career he had a narrow escape, but he carried it with his usual jaunti-ness, and it gave him not even a pause. He was arrested for a hold-up on Hounslow Heath, when he robbed a man of his money and watch. But there was some doubt about the evidence, and he was acquitted. At the first hearing he appeared with an enormous bouquet in his coat, and with blue ribbons decorating his irons. When Sir John Fielding asked if he had anything to say, his jaunty answer was: "I know no more of the matter than you, nor half as much." A few days after his acquittal he went to Bagnigge Wells, dressed

45　The York Stage attacked by Highwaymen in the Eighteenth Century

46 "Visit to an Old Acquaintance"

From a drawing by Thomas Rowlandson

in scarlet coat, white silk stockings and laced hat, and announced himself as Sixteen-String Jack, the highwayman. His conduct was not to the taste of the company, and a number of young men threw him out of the window of the assembly room. In the struggle he lost a ring, which he said was worth a hundred guineas; but it was no matter; a night's work would replace it. He appeared frequently in public places, always elaborately dressed, or over-dressed; and his vanity always led him to announce himself and to enjoy the notice he attracted. He even turned up at Tyburn during an execution, and told the officials round the "tree" that he, more than others, should be allowed to witness the spectacle.

His last exploit was on the road at Ealing, one autumn afternoon, when he robbed the chaplain to Princess Amelia. He was taken, and identified, and at the trial was condemned. He appeared for the trial in a costume of pea-green, a ruffled shirt, and a hat with silver strings. Because he had been once acquitted he thought he might again confuse the evidence, and while the case was being heard he ordered a supper for himself and a few friends, as a celebration. The supper had to be cancelled, but after a short spell of dismay, his arrogance returned; and while waiting his turn in the next batch of executions, he had plenty of company and some agreeable times. On one occasion he had a cell-party of seven girls to dine with him. He died, as they are all said to have done, intrepid to the last.

De Quincey, in his *Autobiographic Sketches*, offers many pictures of English travel in the last years of the century. One point he makes is that very young men, when travelling, rather hoped for an encounter with a highwayman, and kept their pistols primed. But highwaymen seldom interfered with alert young men. Another of his points is that on the roads of his childhood no carriage could ever travel straight. He recalls standing at the front of his mother's carriage, and watching the postillion "quartering"—that is, driving from side to side of the road to avoid the ruts and pot-holes:

> Before you stretched a wintry length of lane, with ruts deep enough to fracture the leg of a horse, filled to the brim with standing pools of rain water; and the collateral chambers of these ruts kept from becoming confluent by thin ridges . . . to maintain the footing upon which, so as not to swerve, was a trial of some skill both for the horses and their postillion. . . . Go to sleep at the beginning of a stage, and the last thing you saw—wake up, and the first thing you saw—was the line of wintry pools, the poor off-horse planting his steps with care, and the cautious postillion gently applying his spur, whilst manœuvring across this system of grooves with some sort of science that looked like a gipsy's palmistry.

1*

Captain Malet, in his *Annals of the Road*, recalls that his great-grandfather, living in Somerset in the later eighteenth century, wished to have a coach built in London, and was obliged to send the coach-builder the measurement between the ruts of his roads, so that the wheels should fit them.

De Quincey's first journey was made when he was nine, in company with a somewhat older boy. They went by post-chaise from Lanca-shire into Lincolnshire. In a nine-hour day they did about forty miles, with four changes of horses. Each change took about half an hour, as against the two-minute changes of thirty years later. The inns he remembered as extremely comfortable:

> What cosy old parlours in those days! low-roofed, glowing with ample fires, and fenced from the blasts of doors by screens, whose foldings were or seemed to be infinite. What motherly landladies! won, how readily, to kindness the most lavish by the mere attractions of simplicity and youthful innocence, and finding so much interest in the bare circumstance of being a traveller at a childish age. Then what blooming young hand-maidens; how different from the knowing and worldly demireps of modern high-roads. And sometimes grey-headed and faithful waiters, how sincere and how attentive, by comparison with their flippant successors.

But the inns were by no means clean, nor did they make provision for the toilet of the guest. Under the beds and in the corners could usually be found accumulations of many years' dust; and chance travellers who wished to wash before meals had no means of doing so. When De Quincey and some others made a practice of asking for a basin and water, they were at first heard with surprise, and were told that the maids were too busy. After repeated requests, they were eventually given one basin of water between them, and that was brought into the breakfast-room. By keeping up their demands at each visit to particular inns, they finally got innkeepers to adopt the practice of providing in the hall a whole row of basins and jugs for the use of coach-passengers.

The treatment given in English inns to foot travellers was still short of common civility, though he says that in Wales it was quite different. In that country no sort of disgrace attached to pedestrian travel, and most of the people he met in Welsh inns, all of them of a "respectable" class, were travelling on foot, and were received without question. But when he reached Shrewsbury on foot, and went to the inn to await the London mail-coach, he was viewed with suspicion until he announced that he was a passenger for the mail, and made no objection when he was escorted to his room with four wax lights. This procedure of supplying the guest with wax candles, for which a charge of five to seven shillings was made, was part of the snobbery of inn life. Guests who objected, and said that ordinary candles would do, were treated with some contempt unless they were so rich that they could afford to be mean. When De Quincey accepted the wax lights, his acceptance overrode the disgrace of having arrived on foot, and he was treated with all civility.

Another touch of snobbery was shown in the different attitudes to the inside passengers of coaches and the outside. The outsides were not allowed to breakfast or dine at the same table as the insides, or even in the same room. He mentions a case where three determined outsides, of as good a standing as the insides, did sit down at the same table as the insides. The insides protested against this outrage, and the head waiter, under pretence of finding the outsides a better table, led them away to the kitchen. On another occasion, when the outsides flatly refused to go among the post-boys in the kitchen, and demanded to be served in the proper dining-room, the waiter arranged a separate table for them at the end of the room, and—set a large screen round it. According to De Quincey, it was the undergraduates of Oxford who put an end to this absurd practice. They made a point of always riding outside, maintaining that it was far preferable to the stuffy inside; that it was, indeed, not the attic, as it had often been called, but the upper drawing-room, and that the inside was the coal-cellar.

Within a year, by their insistent propaganda, the outside had become the fashionable part of the coach, and it was understood that the inside was a place for merchants and common citizens and old women. Thereafter, distinctions dropped, and the coach company, inside and outside, dined at one table.

But a German who travelled in England in 1799, Henry Meister, could not understand the custom of travelling outside a coach. He mentions, as worth mentioning, the fact that he had seen from twelve to fifteen people perched on the top of a coach, and among them some women who appeared to be in good circumstances. He considered it utterly contradictory to the good sense shown in so many matters by the English people. He also considered it dangerous, but remarked that the English traveller seemed indifferent to danger, whether travelling on horseback or by coach. "For this reason it is that we see more wooden legs here than in any other country." A coaching custom that displeased him was the custom, at every change of horses, of being presented with glasses of punch and bowls of brandy and water, "which circulated from one man's mouth so

politely to that of his next neighbour." Another custom he disliked
was one that was common in the sixteenth century, but not so
common, I think, at the end of the eighteenth; though, as a pains-
taking observer, he must have witnessed it. "I did not approve
moreover of the large table-cloths which covered the dining-tables,
and were used to wipe your mouth and fingers in the place of
napkins."

He makes a special point of the traffic to and from London and the
country, and learned that on a certain day of the week no less than
fourteen hundred public vehicles set out from the capital: diligences,
stage-coaches, hackney-coaches, and mail-coaches, some with four
wheels, some with three, and some with eight and ten. The last
were no doubt the waggons, which he describes as built in the shape
of a gondola completely covered, and as carrying thirty to forty
passengers.

At that time, when night travelling by the mails had become the
custom, the roads of England certainly were humming both night
and day. By a wonderfully adjusted time-table, all the mails for
London, from all parts, arrived in London at or around six in the
morning. All through the night they rolled at their steady six miles
an hour along the southern, western, eastern and northern roads,
independent of each other, yet all with a common object. They
rolled along, as it were, the spokes of a wheel, meeting at six o'clock
at its hub, the Post Office in Lombard Street. However many
miles they might be from each other at any given hour of the night,
they came together in that short and narrow but important street
with the precision of destiny.

Traffic was swelling. The coaching age was rising to that golden
age when coaching was not merely a means of transit, but was enjoyed
for its own sake alone. It became a subject of study. Young men
of the aristocracy sought to be proficient in the art of driving four-in-
hand. They paid bribes to sit on the box-seat next to the coachman
and to receive hints from him. The professional coachman became a
hero second only to the pugilist. The young bloods imitated his
dress, his style, his speech. They bought him rum and brandies, and
were highly honoured when they found that he regarded them as
sufficiently apt in the art to move him to break the law and to invite
them to "tool 'em along a bit."

That Golden age, like most Golden Ages, lasted only a decade or
two. To those of that time it looked as though coaching would go
on and on, with even smarter coaches, more spirited horses, finer
turn-outs, smoother roads, and still greater artists of the whip. Then,

47   A Scene outside the "White Lion" at Ponders End, 1802
From a print by Rowlandson

48   Calling Coach Passengers from Breakfast (note the hams hanging
from the tree)
From a print of ca. 1820

49 A well-loaded Stage-Wagon

From a drawing of ca. 1820 by J. L. Agasse

when coaching was at its very peak of perfection, and the roads and the inns were enjoying a bright confusion of life, came, in the next century, a new form of travel; less picturesque, but, at its very slowest, faster than the fastest coach on the road. But before the usurper arrived, the road was to have thirty years of prosperity, and travel at twelve miles an hour was to inspire more than one person with a sense of the glory of motion.

CHAPTER FOUR

Down the Road in Glory

THE FIRST thirty years of the nineteenth century were not only the liveliest years of road travel; they were, until almost the end of the century, the last. But they were thirty years of great days and great doings. They marked the glorification of the road, and for the rest of the century the road-life of those years was recorded and annotated and celebrated in volume after volume. Among the best-known celebrants were Captain Birch-Reynardson, Captain Malet, Stanley Harris, C. J. Apperley ("Nimrod"), Lord William Lennox, Captain Haworth, Edward Corbett. They wrote of the road, and of its incidents of frost and flood and snowdrift, not, as earlier travellers did, in terms of abomination, but in terms expressing nostalgia. They loved it in all its detail, pleasant and unpleasant. They wrote of coachmen and their style with the ribbons. They wrote of the guards and their oddities. They wrote of ostlers and post-boys. They wrote of the sustained speed of ten miles an hour, and of record bursts by which some famous whips made up time lost by a broken trace, and of how those famous whips kept their time at each stage with such punctuality and regularity that local people set their watches by their arrival.

Birch-Reynardson, in his *Down the Road*, apostrophising those who were young when he was young, makes a list of the memorable features of those days of travel:

You will be able to recall the coachmen and the guards, and the very horses you have driven; the foggy mornings out of London; the Peacock at Islington; the pretty barmaid who used to give you your glass of rum and milk; the cold, snowy days and nights you have passed on the mail or coach; the guard and his yard of tin on the mail, wakening up the drowsy toll-bar keeper. . . . You will remember the cheery-keyed bugle of the guard on the coach, upon which he played "Oh, dear, what can the matter be?" or some such lively tune, as he passed through the different towns in the middle of the night. . . . You will have a lively recollection of the bitter cold that pervaded your half-frozen form, and the dire hunger that had taken possession of your inner man. . . . You will, no doubt, remember the look of the streets as you entered London about six o'clock of a winter's morning; how dimly the oil lamps used to burn at that time of day. You will remember the smell of the steam from the horses, as

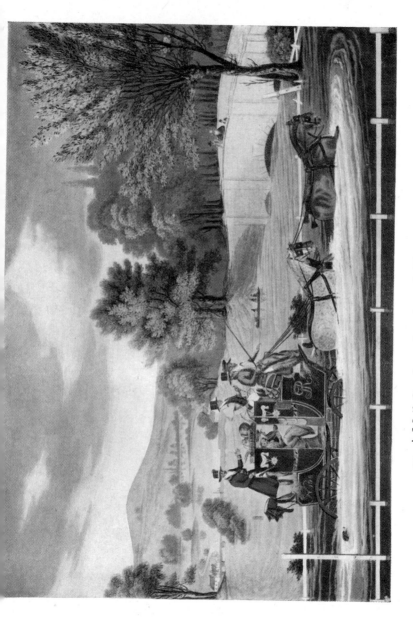

50   A Mail-Coach passing through Flooded Country

From a print of ca. 1820

ROYAL HOTEL COACH OFFICE,
Cheltenham

IMPROVED SAFETY & ELEGANT LIGHT POST COACHES,
DAILY TO THE FOLLOWING PLACES.

LONDON The Magnet Safety Coach. *every Morning at ¼ past Six o'clock thro' Northleach. Burford Witney. Oxford. Henley. Maidenhead. Slough & Hounslow*

LONDON Royal Veteran. *every Morning at ¼ past Eight thro' Northleach. Burford Witney. Oxford. Wycomb & Uxbridge*

OXFORD & LONDON Two Day Coach *every day except Sundays at Twelve o'clock Sleeps at Oxford*

OXFORD Coaches. *every Morning at ¼ past Six & ¼ past Eight o'clock*

BATH The Original Post Coach. *every day except Sundays at Nine o'clock through Gloucester & Rodborough.*

BATH The York House Coach. *every day except Sundays at Two o'clock through Painswick & Stroud.*

BRISTOL The Traveller *every day except Sundays at Twelve o'clock thro' Gloucester & Newport.*

BRISTOL The Royal Pilot. *through Gloucester every Monday Wednesday. & Friday. at ¼ past One o'clock.*

EXETER The Traveller. *every day except Sundays. at Twelve thro' Gloucester. Bristol. Bridgewater. Taunton. Wellington. Collumpton. & Exeter. where it meets Coaches for Plymouth*

GLOUCESTER Accommodation Coaches *every Morning at Nine. ¼ past Nine. & Twelve. o'clock. Afternoon at ¼ past One. Three Five & Seven o'clock in the Evening*

TEWKESBURY Coaches *every Morning except Sundays at Eight & Twelve. Afternoon at ¼ past One. every Evening at 8*

MALVERN The Mercury *every Morning at ¼ before Eight. except Sundays. to Essing to the Hotel. Malvern Wells arrives at Eleven o'clock leaves Malvern at Five*

LIVERPOOL The Magnet. *every Tuesday. Thursday & Saturday. at Twelve o'clock thro' Worcester Birmingham Walsall Stafford. Stone. & Newcastle.*

LIVERPOOL The Aurora *every day except Sundays at ¼ past one o'clock sleeping at Birmingham*

MANCHESTER The Traveller *every day except Sundays at Twelve o'clock thro' Worcester. Sleeping at Birmingham*

SHEFFIELD The Amity *every day except Sundays at Twelve o'clock through Burton. Derby & Chesterfield.*

CHESTER The Dispatch. *every day except Sundays thro' Newport & Fernhill*

BIRMINGHAM The Traveller thro' *Worcester. every day except Sunday. at Twelve o'clock*

BIRMINGHAM The York House Coach *thro' Worcester every day except Sundays at ¼ past One o'clock*

BIRMINGHAM The Mercury. *thro' Worcester every Morning at Eight*

WORCESTER Coaches. *every Morning at Eight & Twelve. also at ¼ past one o'clock. in the Afternoon*

WOLVERHAMPTON The Everlasting *every Morning at Eight. except Sundays*

COVENTRY The Pilot. *thro' Evesham Alcester. Stratford Warwick & Leamington. every day except Sundays at ¼ past one o'clock*

FLY WAGGONS & VANS TO LONDON
on Tuesdays Thursdays & Saturdays at Twelve o'clock & arrives the following Night

THOMAS HAINES Jun.ʳ & Co. — PROPRIETORS
NB Every possible comfort & accommodation afforded to those who may be pleased to honour this Establishment with their patronage

COACHES SENT TO ANY PART OF THE TOWN TO TAKE UP IF REQUIRED

S.Y. Griffith & Co. Copper Plate Printers

A Cheltenham Coaching Notice of *c.* 1820

you passed under the arch of the Swan with Two Necks or into the yard of the Bull and Mouth. . . . You will remember all these little circumstances, and many more that I could name. You will say and think with me, I dare say, that in spite of wet and cold, frost and snow, and all the variations of temperature that one used to go through on a coach, both by day and night, they were jolly times.

It was the Golden Age, the high noon of coaching; and it never declined from noon to sunset. When it ended, it was still at its meridian. It was the age of crack coaches, crack whips, and mettled horses. It was the age of fast coaches whose names have passed into nineteenth-century history: the Shrewsbury "Wonder," the Devonport "Quicksilver," the Manchester "Telegraph," the Brighton "Age," the York "Regent" and "Highflyer," the Birmingham "Tantivy"; coaches which seemed to have a being and a pace of their own independent of what kind of horses might be harnessed to them. There was a passion and precision about the whole business of coaching; something that stirred men's minds and pulses as they are stirred to-day by the perfect car. All sorts of people had something to say about them; not only the experts already named, but the general writers—Hazlitt, De Quincey, Borrow, Thomas Hughes, Dickens, Disraeli, and Cobbett. Coaches and all the matters that attended on coaching moved them to rhapsody. Most of their rhapsodies are well known, but Cobbett's may not be so well known. Cobbett was seldom moved to delight. A well-kept farm might move him, but he found few of them; he was mostly moved to indignation for which his times afforded many occasions. But the mail- and stage-coaches did move him to approbation:

> Next to a fox-hunt the finest sight in England is a stage-coach just ready to start. A great sheep or cattle fair is a beautiful sight; but in a stage-coach you see more of what man is capable of performing. The vehicle itself; the harness, all so complete and so neatly arranged, so strong and clean and good; the beautiful horses, impatient to be off; the inside full, and the outside covered, in every part, with men, women and children, boxes, bags, bundles; the coachman, taking his reins in one hand and the whip in the other, gives a signal with his foot, and away they go, at the rate of seven miles an hour—the population and the property of a hamlet. One of these coaches coming in, after a long journey, is a sight not less interesting. The horses are now all sweat and foam, the reek from their bodies ascending like a cloud. The whole equipage is covered perhaps with dust and dirt. But still, on it comes, as steady as the hand of a clock.

Artists, too, were attracted by the colour and pageantry of coaching, and it was about this period that a whole group appeared whose

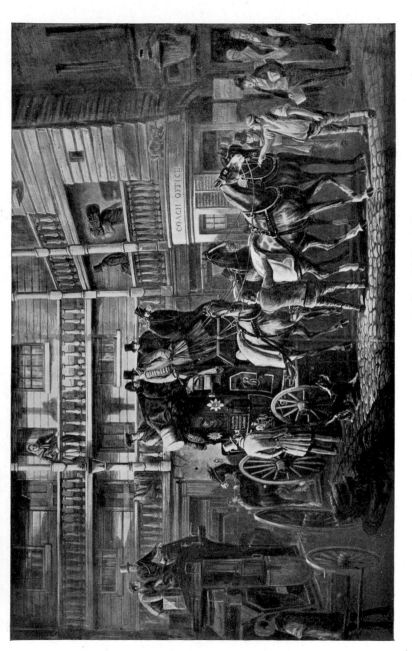

51   The Glasgow Mail leaving the "Bull and Mouth," *ca.* 1830
From a print by Cooper Henderson

52 The Turnpike Gate

From a print by Cooper Henderson

53 "The Sleeping Gatekeeper"

From a print of ca. 1830

names are closely identified with the coach—J. F. Herring (himself a coachman), James Pollard, Henry Alken, John Sturgess, Hanhart, C. B. Newhouse, and Cooper Henderson. Coaching became a pleasure in itself. By many men it was not used for the purpose of going to a particular place. They went week by week, up and down the same road or stretch of road with no interest in their terminus. Their interest was in the performance of the coach, the rapidity of the change, the style and technique of the coachman, and the speed. Byron, in *Don Juan*, satirised this passion. Nothing, he said, gave a man such spirits, or had the effect of adding cayenne to curry:

> As going at full speed—no matter where its
> Direction be, so 'tis but in a hurry,
> And merely for the sake of its own merits;
> For the less cause there is for all this flurry,
> The greater is the pleasure in arriving
> At the great end of travel, which is—driving.

Travellers of this sort went anywhere on any coach that was talked about, either on the character of the coachman or on its speed. They enjoyed great days and nights, and in later years remembered every little incident of those days and nights.

Much of the credit for those great days and great doings was due to two engineers who turned their skill to road-making—Thomas Telford and John Macadam. Between them they remade most of the roads of England and Scotland. The two men had different methods, and each of them had his supporters. But Macadam's method gradually superseded Telford's, and was adopted by authorities everywhere. As De Quincey said, in reference to the increased speed of travel: "It is in reality to Mr. Macadam that we owe it. All the roads in England, within a few years, were remodelled, and upon principles of Roman science. From mere beds of torrents and systems of ruts, they were raised universally to the condition and appearance of gravel walks in private parks."

The sense of speed affected the coach-owners in naming their coaches. They were no longer Machines or Regulators. They were named Highflyers, Quicksilvers, Comets, Rockets, Greyhounds, Lightnings, Expresses, Hirondelles. On May Day of each year, rival coaches working the same road made a race of their journey, stage against mail or stage against stage, Comet against Quicksilver. On those occasions, to lighten the coach, and perhaps to avoid claims for death or injury, they carried no passengers. The passion for speed, of course, led to innumerable accidents, many of them fatal, and sometimes the driver of an overturned coach was indicted for

K*

manslaughter. But Mercury is a planet with great influence upon this planet and its people, and ever since men began to move they have worshipped speed with an anthem whose burden is—Faster, Faster, Faster. In our own time they have reached a speed of two hundred miles an hour, and no doubt it will increase until it defeats itself, and they will go round the world and be back at their starting-point ten seconds after leaving it. Travel will be the same as standing still. But in the Golden Age of coaching they were only just tasting the pleasure of speed, and a few lives here and there did not greatly matter.

But really, the accidents, considering the vast number of coaches and other vehicles on the roads, and their bursts of speed, were very few. Many of the dangers of the last century had been eliminated. The roads were better. The vehicles were of better design. The coachmen were not the drunken incompetent men of the past; they were chosen for their skill. The dangers of being benighted were less. Most of the country was by that time enclosed, and at every few miles there was an inn which, even if it was not a posting inn, was usually ready to receive a horse traveller at any time of night.

Yet with all modern improvements, coach travelling was not much more comfortable than it had been. What had been gained by better appointments, better springs, and better everything else, was lost by rush and hurry. The coaches, mail and stage, stopped at appointed places for breakfast and dinner, but their time-table worked so much to the minute that the stop scarcely gave the passengers time to get anything like a meal. Ten minutes was allowed for breakfast, and for dinner twenty minutes. The guard's horn was supposed to give notice to the inn that the coach was arriving, so that dinner might be on the table at the moment the passengers alighted. If we may accept contemporary accounts, it seldom was. There was often much delay in service, so that while passengers paid the standard half-crown for dinner, they had time for little more than a few mouthfuls, and the same joints would serve the table for three coaches. Sometimes unscrupulous innkeepers bribed the drivers and guard to get the company out, with their "Time's up, gentlemen—can't wait—must go!" some minutes short of the twenty minutes; or ordered the waiters to put the joints in front of the ladies because they were slow carvers.

Travellers who posted, or went on horseback, could, of course, please themselves, and enjoy their meal and their bottle at leisure. But for the coach passengers, all was breathless hurry and consequent dyspepsia, and this affected public manners. They became selfish and irritable. It was every man for himself. This was so much a feature of a coach journey that somebody, wishing to pay a high compliment to the courtly manners of Constable, the painter, could think of nothing higher than: "He was a gentleman even on a coach journey."

Those many glowing accounts of the excellent dinners and fine English fare provided for travellers, were mostly written later in the century by men who were looking back from the railway age, and had forgotten what those inn meals actually were. There is Disraeli's rhapsody:

> What a dinner! What a profusion of substantial delicacies! What mighty and iris-tinted rounds of beef! What vast and marble-veined ribs! What gelatinous veal-pies! What colossal hams! Those are evidently prize cheeses! And how invigorating is the perfume of those various and variegated pickles! Then the bustle emulating the plenty; the ringing of bells, the clash of thoroughfare, the summoning of ubiquitous waiters, and the all-pervading feeling of omnipotence from the guests, who order what they please to the landlord, who can produce and execute everything they can desire.

And there is Thomas Hughes' description of a coach breakfast. The table was covered with the whitest of white cloths and of china, and bore a pigeon-pie, a ham, a round of cold boiled beef; and a waiter came in with a tray of kidneys, and steaks, and eggs and bacon, and toast and muffins, and coffee and tea. And there is Captain Haworth, who tells us that "the coaches dined in those days on the fat of the land," and gives us the menu of a typical coach dinner—a boiled round of beef, a roast loin of pork, a roast aitchbone of beef, a boiled hand of pork, a roast goose and a boiled leg of mutton.

But contemporary accounts, written in the actual coaching days, differ a little from those eulogies. One writer of the time refers to "the usual coach dinner—a coarse, fat leg of mutton, roasted to a cinder, a huge joint of boiled beef, underdone, and gritty cabbage." Surtees, in one of his Jorrocks sketches in the *New Sporting Magazine*, applies his usual acidulous tone to a description of a coach dinner. The truth probably lay somewhere between him and Disraeli:

> Our travellers had been driven through the passage into a little, dark, dingy room at the back of the house, with a dirty, rain-bespattered window, looking against a whitewashed blank wall. The table, which was covered with a thrice-used cloth, was set out with lumps of bread, knives, and two and three pronged forks laid alternately. Altogether it was anything but inviting, but coach passengers are very complacent; and on the Dover road it matters little if they are not. Coats No. 1, No. 2, and No. 3 are taken

off in succession, for some people wear top-coats to keep out the heat; chins are released from their silken jeopardy, hats are hid in corners. Inside passengers eye outside ones with suspicion. . . . Presently the two dishes of pork, a couple of ducks, and a lump of half-raw, sadly mangled cold roast beef, with waxy potatoes and overgrown cabbages were scattered along the table. "What a beastly dinner!" exclaims an inside dandy in a sable-collared frock; "the whole place reeks with onions and vulgarity." . . . "Now harkee, waiter, there's the guard blowing his horn, and we have scarcely had a bite apiece," cries Mr. Jorrocks, as that functionary sounded his instrument most energetically in the passage; "blow me tight if I stir."

Lord William Lennox, in his recollections of coach travel, is another critic of coach dinners, which he contrasts bitterly with the very excellent dinners he had when on the road in his own carriage. The coach dinner he describes as scalding soup (stained warm water), tough steaks, Scotch collops, underdone boiled leg of mutton, potatoes hot without and hard within; and no time in which to eat it even if it were eatable.

Off the busy roads, things were a little easier. "Nimrod," in his little work on *The Road*, has a story of a Shrewsbury Highflyer, which left Shrewsbury at eight o'clock in the morning to go to Chester, a distance of forty miles, and arrived there at about eight in the evening. He explains how the time was occupied. There were no breakdowns or sick horses; the cause of the leisurely journey was an accommodating coachman. If a bagman wanted to do business at Ellesmere, the coach waited while he did it. If a gentleman, a box-seat passenger, wanted to pay a call on a friend, he was allowed time for it. In the pork-pie season, and apparently Shropshire made some good pork-pies, there would be a half-hour stop at some farmer's home for the eating of one. At Wrexham the coach dined, but it was not a matter of twenty minutes cut down to fifteen by the guard's horn. The driver usually allowed two hours for dinner, and even then did not insist on an exact two hours. He would poke his head in at the door, and announce that the coach was ready—"but don't let me disturb you if you wish for another bottle." The coach, of course, was not a mail.

Towards foot travellers the inn was no more friendly than it had been in the past. It was assumed that if a man was so down as to travel on foot, it would do him no harm to sleep under the hedge; or he might find an ale-house where he could get a shakedown, or sleep in the barn. He could hardly expect his betters at the inn to contaminate themselves with his company. But the ale-house was

54 Stopping the Mail in a Rainstorm

From a print by R. G. Reeve

55 A Post-chaise in Difficulties

From a print by R. G. Reeve

56   Driving a High Gig, 1856
From a print by Newhouse

57   "Just in Time"
From a print by Henry Alken

seldom able to provide food, so usually the foot traveller had to take a meal in the kitchen of the inn, and, like Pastor Moritz, at bed-time be turned out into the night. Samuel Bamford, an intelligent leader of the workers, and one of the organisers of that Manchester meeting of 1819 which, from the massacre by the military, became known as Peterloo, had to come to London after that affair, to surrender to his bail. He made the journey on foot, and had a thoroughly unpleasant time.

Repeatedly when he reached an inn, and asked for a bed, he was put off with the story that the place was full of soldiers and all rooms occupied. At Woburn he was not even allowed to buy a glass of ale. When he entered the inn at that place, nobody took any notice of him beyond a suspicious glance. At last he stopped one of the maids, and asked for a glass of ale. He was told that they did not entertain foot travellers. He expressed surprise, and stated that he was able and willing to pay for whatever he ordered. He was told that it made no difference; the house did not serve any people who travelled on foot. In the account of his journey, which he wrote many years later, he commented on the incident by wondering whether the people of that inn were still in business, and whether, "like scores of their arrogant brotherhood," they had been sufficiently humbled by the railways to be willing at last to sell a cup of ale to a decent way-farer.

After he had suffered many refusals every night of a bed, he found at last a means of getting one. An experience at Northampton gave him the idea, which he passed on to those readers who might some time be in a similar position. At two places he was refused on the plea of billeted soldiers. At a third place to which he was directed, a quite ordinary place where coachmen and guards slept, he was again refused on the same plea:

> It was getting late and almost dark, and I determined not to be shuffled out of this next place by any pretence. . . . I asked the landlady, a smart but unassuming woman, if I could have a bed for this night. From the moment I entered she had been eyeing me over, and seeing, as I suppose, my shoes all dust, and myself a brown and not a very polished-looking character, she said she was very sorry, but there was not a bed to spare in the house, so many soldiers had bought billets. Requesting she would serve me with a pint of ale, I sat down.

When the ale came, he asked for a pipe and tobacco, which were brought. He then asked if he could have a chop or steak, and called for another pint. He sat talking with the farmers in the bar parlour until his supper was brought. After supper, he ordered brandy and hot water, and when he had had more talk and finished his brandy, he called the landlady to bring his bill, observing that it was time he looked out for a lodging. Whereupon the landlady told him to make himself comfortable; that he seemed to be very good company, and that she would find him a bedroom somehow. From that experience he learned how to handle the situation when travelling on foot:

> A foot traveller, if he is really desirous to obtain lodgings, should never stand asking about them. He should walk into a good room—never into the common tap-room—put his dusty feet under a table, ring the bell pretty smartly, and order something to eat and drink, and not speak in the humblest of tones. He will be served quickly and respectfully—that is, if those two things happen to be understood at the house. After his repast he should take his pipe or cigar if he be a smoker, and whether he be or not, he should drink, chat, and make himself quite at ease until bed-time, when all he has to do will be to call the chamber-maid and ask her to light him to bed. That will be done as a matter of course, and he will probably have saved himself a tramp round the town in search of lodgings, and probably, after all, the making of his own bed under a manger or in a hay-loft.

So great was the business of the road in the 1820's that at one place, Hounslow, which was the first western change out of London and the last change in, the inns kept, for coaching and posting, two thousand five hundred horses. At all principal towns where changes were made a similar number was kept. As the upkeep of each horse, according to Lord William Lennox, cost two pounds a week, this meant that in the matter of horses alone, five thousand pounds circulated in each of those towns every week. Some inns on the road kept horses only for private posting, and he mentions two post-masters in one town each of whom stabled three hundred pairs of horses. There were then about sixty mail-coaches on the road, and some hundreds of stage-coaches. Wherever a stage-coach ran, on main roads or cross-country, there was always an opposition coach; sometimes two. They raced each other; they tried to snatch each other's passengers; they competed in fares and speed until, sooner or later, one ran the other off the road.

The coachmen of the royal mails were, as I say, important personages. To share the box-seat with them, and to be honoured by their conversation and their acceptance of one of your cigars, was a privilege which flattered not only the young and gay. The stage-coachmen were not quite of the same quality. The men of the mails were usually young, slim, with whipcord muscles and a perfect seat; and they dressed quietly and neatly. The men of the stage-coaches went rather the other way—towards obesity and loud clothes. Tony Wellers, in fact. Washington Irving has sketched the type:

He has commonly a broad, full face, curiously mottled with red, as if the blood had been forced by hard feeding into every vessel of the skin; he is swelled into jolly dimensions by frequent potations of malt liquors, and his bulk is still further increased by a multiplicity of coats, in which he is buried like a cauliflower. . . . He wears a broad-brimmed, low-crowned hat; a huge roll of coloured handkerchief about his neck, knowingly knotted and tucked in at the bosom; and has in summer-time a large bouquet of flowers in his button-hole; the present, most probably, of some enamoured country lass. His waistcoat is commonly of some bright colour, striped, and his small-clothes extend far below the knees, to meet a pair of jockey-boots which reach about half-way up his legs. . . .

He enjoys great consequence and consideration along the road. . . . When off the box, his hands are thrust into the pockets of his great coat, and he rolls about the inn yard with an air of the most absolute lordliness. Here he is generally surrounded by an admiring throng of ostlers, stable-boys, shoeblacks, and those nameless hangers-on that infest inns and taverns. . . . These all look up to him as to an oracle; treasure up his cant phrases; echo his opinions about horses and other topics of jockey-lore; and, above all, endeavour to imitate his air and carriage.

George Borrow's opinion of stage-coachmen was somewhat different. He did not see them with the sentimental eye which the American brought to English institutions. He described them as low fellows, who were flattered by the attentions of the nobility, "so that these fellows, being low fellows, very naturally thought no small liquor of themselves." He spoke of their brutality and inso-lence; of their way of *demanding* a tip from each passenger at the end of their stage; of their derisive acceptance of a shilling where they were accustomed to receive half-crowns. He rejoiced in their disappearance and loathed their memory.

Improved roads not only increased the number of public coaches, but also the number of private vehicles. Thanks to Macadam, these were of many styles and of much lighter build. They were made for speed. Among them were the phaeton, the curricle, the gig, the whiskey, the stanhope, the tilbury, and the dennet. But with all this dash there were many occasions when travellers found themselves back in the fifteenth century. Macadam's roads were good only when they could be used. Their quality availed nothing when they lay under four feet of snow. And snowstorms, in the early years of the century, were frequent.

L

Often, during winter, all communication was stopped. When the mail-coach was stuck in a snowdrift, the guard would try to go ahead with the mail-bags on horseback, or even on foot. The rule was that His Majesty's mails stopped for nothing. On one or two occasions of this kind the guard lost his life. One Christmas night the Dover mail could get no farther than Canterbury; the road in some places had a depth of snow above the height of the coach. But the mails went on. They were taken from Canterbury to Dover by sledge, drawn by three horses in single file. Passengers were allowed to travel on those sledges at a fare of two pounds. .

Two or three occasions are reported of a coach being stuck deep in a snowdrift, and the coachman and the guard taking the horses and carrying the mails to the nearest town by way of the fields, while the passengers made themselves comfortable as best they could. On one occasion, when a mail-coach without passengers was snow-bound, the coachman went on with the mails, while the guard stayed with the coach. Snow was falling heavily, and during the night it covered the coach. When the guard was dug out he was dead.

In normal times, the speed of both mail- and stage-coaches was so regulated and timed that, in a journey of three hundred miles, with stops for meals and changes, every minute lost had to be made up on the road, so that the coach should maintain its honour and arrive exactly on time. A coach-owner, who ran a coach from London to the west, had his drivers and guards so drilled that he offered to pay to some local charity a sum of eightpence for every minute that his coach was over its time. While the owner of a London–Brighton coach offered, if his coach did not keep time, to return his passengers their fare. The very opposite of our railways, who state on their tickets, which you have to buy with real money, that they don't undertake to carry you anywhere or do anything for you whatever except sell you a ticket.

On a road on which three or four rival services ran—such as the Brighton road, for which twenty coaches left London every day—the time was cut to the half-minute. At the changes, there was no time for the passengers to get down and stretch their limbs. As the guard sounded his horn a furlong away, the fresh team was brought out, and was ready waiting before the coach had pulled up. There was no time, Birch-Reynardson says, for slipping into the bar and getting a glass of something and a biscuit and cheese. The barmaid brought a few things out on a tray, and handed them up to the passengers, but there was no time to exchange gallantries with her. There was time only to swallow a glass of ale, and to snatch from the

58 Snowed up! A Mail-Coach caught in a Blizzard
From a print by Pollard

59 Passengers taking shelter in a Farmhouse after a Mail-Coach Mishap
From a print by Pollard

60 The Four-in-Hand Club, Hyde Park
From a print by Pollard of ca. 1840

61 An Arrival at Melton Mowbray
From a print by Dean Paul

62 Bilking a London "Jarvie"

tray some bread and cheese to eat as you went along; and then you were off again. By night as well as day each coach tried to keep the opposition in sight. When the one ahead saw the lights of the rival catching him up, he would get the guard to hang a coat over the rear-boot lamp of his own coach, so that the rival should not see how far ahead he was.

Most travellers of the time make complaints about coach company. There was always the fat man, who should have engaged two seats; or the talkative man, or the querulous woman. Lord William Lennox said that he once heard a man say that some of his most pleasant acquaintances were people he had met on stage-coaches; from which he deduced that the man must have been singularly fortunate in his coach company or singularly unfortunate in his general acquaintance. The talkative man, suffering from ingrowing conversation, was found in every coach. Lamb's crushing of one of this type is well known, but may still be new to some. He was travelling from Bury St. Edmunds to London with his young ward, Emma Isola:

We travelled with one of those troublesome fellow passengers in a stage-coach, that is called a well-informed man. For twenty miles we discoursed about the properties of steam, probabilities of carriage by ditto, till all my science, and more than all, was exhausted, and I was thinking of escaping my torment by getting up on the outside when, getting into Bishop's Stortford, my gentleman, spying some farming land, put an unlucky question to me: "What sort of crop of turnips do you think we shall have this year?" Emma's eyes turned to me, to know what in the world I could have to say; and she burst into a violent fit of laughter, maugre her pale, serious cheeks, when, with the greatest gravity, I replied: "It depends, I believe, upon boiled legs of mutton." . . . I am afraid my credit sank very low with my fellow traveller, who had thought he had met with a *well-informed* passenger, which is an accident so desirable in a stage-coach.

Travellers on horseback or by post-chaise fared, as I say, much better than coach travellers, either stage or mail. The inns laid themselves out to serve the post travellers, and, of course, made them pay. Where the coach dinner was half a crown, the private traveller paid six or seven shillings; but he did get something a good deal better than the coach dinner. Some inns, such as the Red Lion at Barnet; the Bush at Staines; the Crown at Hounslow, were posting-houses only, and did not cater for the poor coach traveller. The great god Snob was very potent in the world of travel. Mrs. Jennings, in *Sense and Sensibility*, asks a young lady how she travelled to London.

L*

and is answered: "Not in the stage, I assure you. We came post all the way." Posting-houses were the aristocracy of inns, and the dinner at six or seven shillings would usually be a soup; then eels or some other freshwater fish; a roast fowl; lamb cutlets or a saddle of Southdown; bread, cheese and salad. If the season was winter, there was the usual "extra" of two shillings for wax lights. The guest was also expected to take wine with his dinner, and, after dinner, a bottle of port, probably bottled that morning—seven shillings. No doubt many a guest, as Dickens put it, having ordered a bottle of port for the good of the house, drank brandy and water for his own. Posting-houses regarded all who posted as necessarily rich, just as, at the beginning of the motoring age, all innkeepers regarded motorists as rich and therefore to be stung. Breakfast at the posting-house was three shillings. Tea, with a slice or two of thin bread and butter, was two shillings. That was in the 1820's, when one shilling had the spending value of four of ours.

All travellers speak of the expense of posting. The German princeling, Pückler Muskau, who visited England in 1826, found our posting inns "neat and well-attended." They were clean, convenient, and even elegant, and he noted that a traveller is never invited, as in German inns, to eat, sit and sleep in the same room. Still, "travelling is, on the whole, very expensive—especially the posting (which is exactly four times as much as with us) and the fees which you are expected to be giving all day long, in all directions, to every species of servant and attendant." He was a sharp observer, as this passage, on the behaviour of the travelling Englishman, shows:

> Englishmen who do not belong to the aristocracy, and are not very rich, usually travel without a servant by the mail- or stage-coach, which deposits them at the inn. The man who waits on strangers to the coach, cleans their boots, etc., has the universal appellation of Boots. It is, accordingly, Boots who brings your slippers, helps you to pull off your boots, and then departs, first asking at what time you will have, not, as in Germany, coffee, but your hot water to shave. He appears with it punctually at the appointed hour, and brings your clothes cleanly brushed. The traveller then hastens to dress himself and to return to his beloved coffee-room, where the ingredients of breakfast are richly spread upon the table. To this meal he seems to bring more animation than to any other, and, indeed, I think, more appetite; for the number of cups of tea, the masses of bread and butter, eggs and cold meat which he devours awaken silent envy in the breast, or rather in the stomach of the less capable foreigner. He is now not only permitted, but enjoined (by custom, his gospel) to read. At every cup of tea he unfolds a newspaper of the size of a

table-cloth. Not a single speech, crim. con., murder or other catastrophe, invented by the accident-maker in London, escapes him.

Like one who would rather die of a surfeit than leave anything uneaten which he had paid for, the systematic Englishman thinks that, having called for a newspaper, he ought not to leave a letter of it unread. By this means his breakfast lasts several hours, and the sixth or seventh cup is drunk cold. I have seen this glorious meal protracted so long that it blended with dinner; and you will hardly believe me when I assure you that a light supper followed at midnight without the company quitting the table.

He also noted, what English travellers of the time noted, that as you went out of London you found an increasing deterioration. The inns were less comfortable, the post-horses were worse, the postillions more dirty, the dress of the people less respectable, and the charges much higher.

A French visitor of a little later, Baron d'Haussez, in his *La Grande Bretagne* (quoted by John Ashton in his *Reign of William IV*) expressed much the same views as the German. The taste for travelling, he said, which was an expensive taste in any country, was in England truly ruinous, and though it was attended by everything that could give pleasure, the pleasure was cancelled by the drain on the purse. (The French were as frugal then as now.) He noted the prevalence among the young fashionables of the habit of travelling outside the coach, but mistook the reason for their preferring the box-seat:

The desire to breathe fresh air, rather than economic considerations, induce even the richest English to give a preference to outside places. The place most in request—one knows not wherefore—is to the left of the coachman; it is considered as the place of honour and is reserved for fashionables, and even for lords, who do not disdain to travel thus. The sole advantages, which such a station appeared to me to present were the being placed near a well-dressed coachman, and the escaping the chance of travelling by the side of a butcher, a shoemaker or some other individual of that class.

The real reason was the chance of being allowed to "put 'em along a bit." It was a time when coaching had reached perfection in all its points—vehicles, horses, harness, driving skill, and speed—and the observer spoke highly of their turn-out:

The appointments of an English coach are no less elegant than its form. A portly looking coachman seated on a very high coach-box, well-dressed, wearing white gloves, a nosegay in his button-hole, and his chin enveloped in an enormous cravat, drives four horses perfectly matched and harnessed, and as carefully groomed as when they excited admiration in the carriages of Grosvenor and Berkeley Squares. . . . Four-horse coaches are to be seen rapidly traversing the most populous streets of London, without occasioning the least accident, without being at all inconvenienced in the midst of the numerous carriages, which hardly leave the necessary space to pass. . . . In England, where everything is so well arranged, where each person knows so well how to confine himself to the exigencies of his position, the horses do better what they have to do than the horses of other countries, and that, too, without the need of brutal correction.

He spoke of our inns as being among the wonders of English civilisation. He praised the buildings themselves; the efficient servants who, in the larger places, wore livery; the master of the house, whose decent dress indicated a feeling of respect towards his guests; the well-furnished dining-rooms; the meals, whose simplicity of cooking was covered by the quality of the meat and the richness of the plate; and, in short, everything about them except—the exorbitant bills.

He found our postillions smart and accomplished, and noted that they were all men of small stature and light weight. Postillions (or post-boys, as they were called, though many of them were grey-haired) had a livery of their own. This was a short jacket of blue or yellow, a shiny white hat, white cord breeches, top-boots, white stock, and yellow waistcoat with pearl buttons. At all the posting-houses, horses in pairs were kept ready in harness day and night, and the post-boys themselves had to be fully dressed during the day if they were the "next turn-out." Most houses kept ten or a dozen post-boys, who went out in rotation. Stanley Harris, in his *Old Coaching Days*, quotes a set of printed rules that hung in the yard of a famous posting-house. One of them was "That the first and second turn post-boy shall be always booted and spurred, with their horses ready harnessed, from eight o'clock in the morning until seven o'clock at night."

Some of the posting-houses supplied the post-chaise as well as the horses. Lord William Lennox describes what he calls "hack-chaises" as no fair substitute for one's own. They were not very well hung on their springs; the windows seldom fitted, but rattled all the way along like a dice-box; the floor was covered with enough straw to hold a covey of partridges; and though the vehicles were light and ran smoothly, there was the trouble of transferring your luggage to a new one at every stage. He thought the perfect mode of travelling was in your own post-chaise or britchka.

Cobbett differed from him. There was no pleasure, he held, in travelling, except on horseback or on foot. Carriages merely took

63 An Inn Yard, *ca.* 1840
From a contemporary print

64 A Fire in an Inn Yard
From a print by Rowlandson

65 "The Road to a Fight," 1821

your body from place to place; and if you wanted merely to be "conveyed" they were good enough for that; but they gave you no chance of seeing or knowing anything of the country through which you passed. But he was no great friend to general travelling. He found a woman in a Hampshire village, a woman of about thirty, who had never been more than two miles from her village, and he found her as acute and sensible as anybody else. Which led him to the reflection that the facilities which then existed (1826) of moving human bodies from place to place were "among the curses of the country the destroyers of industry, of morals, and of happiness."

Cobbett not only wrote *Advice to Young Men*. At various points of the *Rural Rides* he offered advice to those whose affairs compelled them to travel. One of his points was that one would get on better by taking very little food and drink. On many of his rides he had no breakfast and no dinner. He set out one morning and rode thirty miles before breaking his fast. Sometimes, in a whole day, he took only a slice of meat and a slice of bread, which he ate at midday in the saddle. The money he saved by not eating or drinking on his rides he gave away to poor people he met on the road. "I know well that I am the better for not stuffing and blowing myself out, and with the savings I make many and many a happy boy; and now and then I give a whole family a good meal with the cost of a breakfast or a dinner that would have done me mischief." He never ate more than twice a day, and never ate meat later than about one o'clock midday. At his usual bed-time, he took a little milk and water, and at eight o'clock he went to bed. Breakfast found him hungry, but he ate only a small portion of cold meat and bread, and he never touched what he called "garden stuff."

Forty or forty-five miles a day was a common journey with him. Often he had to do more, since he disliked turnpike roads, and would try to cut across country, and would lose his way. Nobody seemed to understand his dislike of turnpike roads:

> In cases like mine, you are pestered to death to find out the way to set out, to get from place to place. The people you have to deal with are innkeepers, ostlers, and post-boys; and they think you mad if you express your wish to avoid turnpike roads; and a great deal more than half-mad if you talk of going, even from necessity, by any other road. They think you a strange fellow if you will not ride six miles on a turnpike road, rather than two on any other road.

On one of the rides he got into a pretty fix because of his determination not to go over Hindhead. With the help of an incompetent guide, he got lost, wet, and benighted, and found himself after all on Hindhead. He wanted to get to Thursley from Hambledon. Thursley lay at the foot of Hindhead, on the other side, but he wanted to get to it on the flat:

> I had been over that sweet Hindhead, and had seen too much of turnpike road and of heath to think of taking another so large dose of them. I knew it was about five miles from Headley to Thursley; and I therefore resolved to go to Headley, in spite of all the remonstrances of friends, who represented to me the danger of breaking my neck at Hawkley and of getting buried in the bogs of Woolmer Forest.

The route he planned was through East Meon, Froxfield, Hawkley, Greatham, and over Woolmer Forest to Headley. Everybody advised him not to attempt to go down the hanger of Hawkley, but he did it. He had to dismount, and let his horse go down alone. It went partly on its feet and partly on its hocks. The way was extremely slippery, and he himself was only able to get down by holding on to branches of the undergrowth. Having got down, he had a river to cross, but he managed this and reached Hawkley. There he asked the way to Thursley, and was shown the road over Hindhead. He said he wanted to go round it. He was advised not to, but when he persisted, the farmer of whom he had inquired put him on the way to the road to Greatham. He got to Greatham and across Woolmer Forest, and at last reached Headley, wondering whether he had ever, in England or America, seen worse roads. Between Greatham and Headley, he repeatedly asked the way to Thursley, and became quite petulant when everybody told him he must go by Liphook. "These people seemed to be posted at all these stages to turn me aside from my purpose, and to make me go over that Hindhead which I had resolved to avoid."

At Headley, which he reached at dusk, he stopped at the Holly Bush, as he had eaten nothing since eight o'clock that morning. He had some cold bacon and bread, and then decided to push on. There was a moon, but there was also rain, and the moonlight was faint; so he hired a man, for three shillings, to guide him to the foot of Hindhead, and left a comfortable fire, and set out. The guide wore a white smock frock, so that he might be seen:

> We trotted on pretty fast for about half an hour; when I perceived, not without some surprise, that the rain, which I knew to be coming from the south, met me full in the face, when it ought, according to my reckoning, to have beat upon my right cheek. I called the guide repeatedly to ask him if he was sure that he was right, to which he always answered "Oh, yes, sir, I know the road." At last, after going about six miles in a southern direction, the guide turned short to the left. That brought the rain

upon my right cheek, and though I could not account for the long stretch to the south, I thought that at any rate we were *now* in the right track; and after going about a mile in this new direction, I began to ask the guide how much further we had to go; for I had got a pretty good soaking, and was rather impatient to see the foot of Hindhead.

In lifting his head to speak to the guide he saw that they were on the brow of a steep hill, and that the guide had begun to descend. He himself, seeing that the hill was so steep and that his saddle was so wet, dismounted to lead his horse down, when the guide confessed that he had lost his way. The only thing to do was to turn back. On the way back they met two men who showed them the way they ought to go. They went that way for about a mile, and at last came out on the turnpike road:

Not, indeed, at the *foot*, but on the tip-top of that very Hindhead on which I had so repeatedly vowed I would not go. We came out on the turnpike some hundred yards on the Liphook side of the buildings called The Hut; so that we had the whole of three miles of hill to come down at not much better than a foot pace, with a good pelting rain at our backs.

This led him to reflect on the good fire and the scene he had left at the inn at Headley. He had left a room full of men in smock frocks, drinking and smoking and talking, and he, who was then dry and warm, had moralised on their folly in spending their time in such a way. But after descending Hindhead, and reaching an inn at the foot, with his skin soaking and his teeth chattering, he decided that those men were "the wisest assembly I had ever set eyes on. A real Collective Wisdom." When Cobbett was in a bad temper, somebody usually felt it. In this case, his "guide" felt it. Cobbett refused to pay him his three shillings:

"Either," said I, "you did not know the way well, or you did; if the former, it was dishonest in you to undertake to guide me: if the latter, you have wilfully led me miles out of my way." He grumbled; but off he went. He certainly deserved nothing; for he did not know the way, and he prevented some other man from earning and receiving the money. But, had he not caused me to *get upon Hindhead*, he would have had the three shillings. I had, at one time, got my hand in my pocket; but the thought of having been beaten pulled it out again.

Travel, it will be seen, away from the main roads, still had its dangers. The crossing of the sands of the estuaries still led to annual fatalities. Early in the century a stage-coach overturned on the Lancaster sands, which, in places, were quicksands. The passengers hung on to the coach until, two by two, they were taken off by the

M

horses and carried back to the shore. Soon after the last passenger was taken off the coach disappeared into the sands. In the eighteen-thirties another coach was sucked into the same sands, again without loss of life; but a few years later, on a Whit Monday, a holiday group, crossing the sands in a cart, went off the safe track, and were drawn with the cart into the sands and seen no more. The sands between Bamborough and Holy Island and Berwick also claimed their victims; and on the road itself there was often, in seasons of heavy rain, the danger of drowning.

On a foggy night of 1827, a coach approaching Hounslow got off the road into a pond, and a box-seat passenger was flung off and drowned. When a coach from a seaside town was loading up on the quay, one of the horses became restless, and, plunging forward, carried the coach over the edge. Two women, inside passengers, were drowned. A more serious affair happened at a west country port in somewhat similar circumstances; on that occasion ten of the passengers were drowned. Again, a coach going from Cheltenham to Hereford, on a night of heavy rain, when streams and rivers were overflowing, came to a bridge whose supports had been worn down by the rush of water. The weight of the coach completely broke the bridge, and the coachman, the guard, and a passenger were flung into the river. They were not drowned; they supported themselves all night by clinging to rocks; but soon after their rescue in the early morning, the passenger died. Apart from the dangers of snow and flood, there were the other dangers arising from reckless coachmen, runaway horses, collisions, and the collapse of a wheel or axle-tree. But with the vast number of vehicles tearing along the roads in opposition, the wonder is that disasters were not even more than they were.

On certain occasions in the first fifteen years of the century, the coaches went down from London not only in their usual bravery of gleaming harness and coloured wheels, but dressed with flags and laurels announcing military or naval victory. They went down in glory. As De Quincey said:

The mail-coach it was that distributed over the face of the land, like the opening of apocalyptic vials, the heart-shaking news of Trafalgar, of Salamanca, of Vittoria, of Waterloo. . . . Heads of every age crowd to the windows—young and old understand the language or our victorious symbols—and rolling volleys of sympathising cheers run along us, behind us, and before us. The beggar, rearing himself against the wall, forgets his lameness—real or assumed—thinks not of his whining trade, but stands erect with bold, exulting smiles as we pass him. Women and children, from garrets alike and cellars, through infinite London, look down or look

66 "A [Fanciful] View in Whitechapel Road, 1830"

67 "The New Steam Carriage," 1828

68 "Sir Charles Dance's Steam Carriage"

up with loving eyes upon our gay ribbons and our martial laurels; sometimes kiss their hands; sometimes hang out, as signals of affection, pocket-handkerchiefs, aprons, dusters . . .

At Christmas, too, the horses were rosetted, and their collars and heads dressed with holly, and the sides of the coach with mistletoe. The roof, and the fore and hind boots were crammed with parcels and hampers, and the whole coach was festooned with turkeys, and hares and other game, and oyster barrels. Many coaches, on the two days before Christmas, carried no passengers. They could do better, financially, by using all seats, inside and out, for parcels. The top of the coach was usually so laden with hampers, and bags and boxes, held down by a tarpaulin, that there was only just room on the box-seat for the coachman, and the guard was wedged into his seat at the rear, with a mountain of luggage before him and another heap all round him.

But the great day for the coaches was May Day. Each coach and its horses were decked with ribbons and flowers. The coachman's whip was twined with flowers, and the guard had a similar decoration to his yard-of-tin. Each of them wore an enormous bouquet. The horses' necks were wreathed in blossom, and the sides of the coach were draped with boughs and evergreens. At various places along the road, the coaches were halted by the townspeople, and young girls offered to coachmen, guards, and passengers, trays of wines and pastries. This custom went back to the early eighteenth century, when the coaches laid up for the winter. On May Day they reappeared, and as their first passage of the year coincided with the return of light and warmth, they were given a special greeting. In later times they ran all through the year, and they had no special relation to May Day. But the people seemed to enjoy their little celebration, and in some places it was kept up till the end of the coaching age.

The most famous of these celebrations was that of Sutton-on-Trent, on the Great North Road. It lasted for a whole week from May Day. The town was decked with greenery, and as each decked coach came in it had to stop while young girls in spotless aprons, with damask-covered trays, plied the passengers with home-made refreshments. The trays bore jam-tarts, plum-cakes, gingerbread, biscuits, and new bread; and the liquids were home-brewed ale, currant, gooseberry, and parsnip wine, and cherry brandy and other cordials. Everybody, as a matter of courtesy, took something, with the result that the landlord of the inn where the coach dined found that his dishes were let off lightly enough to serve three or four coaches.

M*

An affair of that Corinthian age that always crowded the roads with anything that went on wheels was a Mill or Turn-Up. Boxing meetings were actually illegal, if held on public ground, but they were seldom broken up. Now and then a sour magistrate would get word of a forthcoming meeting, and would send the constables to proclaim it; but generally the meetings were winked at, and often the local magistrates themselves were, as private sportsmen, present at the meeting. The rendezvous was kept a secret until the day before the meeting, and then was passed to the Lads of the Fancy by word of mouth. There were certain centres in the large towns where such information could be had. Sometimes, when the promoters heard that the magistrates were aware of the meeting, the rendezvous would be changed two or three times on the last day.

A good picture of the road out of London on the morning of a fight is given by Pierce Egan:

> By this time Piccadilly was all in motion—coaches, carts, gigs, tilburies, whiskies, buggies, dog-carts, sociables, dennets, curricles and sulkies were passing in rapid succession, intermingled with tax-carts and waggons decorated with laurel, conveying company of the most varied description. In a few minutes, the barouche being at the door, crack went the whip, and off they bowled. Here was to be seen the dashing Corinthian, tickling up his tits and his bang-up set-out of blood and bone, giving the go-by to a heavy drag laden with eight brawny bull-faced blades, smoking their way down behind a skeleton of a horse, to whom in all probability a good feed of corn would have been a luxury; pattering among themselves, occasionally chaffing the more elevated drivers by whom they were surrounded. There was a waggon, full of all sorts upon the lark, succeeded by a donkey-cart with four insides. . . . Travelling gently along the road, they were presently impeded by a crowd of persons who surrounded a long cart or waggon, which had just been overturned, and had shot out a motley group of personages who were being lifted on their legs, growling and howling. The next object of attraction was a small cart drawn by one poor animal, sweating and snorting under the weight of six Swells.

Many of the company, on those occasions, were not in the secret of the rendezvous. They just followed their leader, and were never sure that they were on the right road until they saw one of the principals or some well-known patron of the Ring. On this particular journey everybody followed everybody else, and hoped for the best. Only when they saw Randall coming along in his gig were they satisfied:

> Mirth and merriment appeared spread over every countenance, though expectation and anxiety were intermingled here and there in the features of the real lads of the fancy; many of whom had bets to a considerable

amount depending upon the result of the day. The bang-up blades were
pushing their prads along in gay style. The queer fancy lads, who had
hired hacks from the livery-stable keepers, were kicking up a dust, while
the neck-or-nothing boys, with no prospect but a Whereas before their
eyes, were as heedless of their personal safety as they were of their creditor's
property. Jaded hacks and crazy vehicles were to be seen on all sides;
dust flying, women sprawling, men bawling, dogs barking. . . .

The favourite places for meetings in the London district were
Hertfordshire and Sussex. Wade's Mill, near Ware, was the scene of
many contests, but many more were held at Blindley Heath, Copthall
Common, or Crawley Down. On the morning of a fight, and through
the day before, the roads round about those places, and the neighbouring inns, were crowded. The crowd came not only from London,
but from Brighton, Worthing, and other coast towns. The inns of
Godstone, East Grinstead, Reigate, Bletchingley, were occupied to
the doors on the preceding night, and innkeepers could charge what
they liked not for a room, or even for a bed, but for a share in a bed
with perhaps two bed-fellows. But according to Pierce Egan, little
sleep was to be had. Vehicles of every description were passing
through those towns all night. Most of the crowd sat in the down-
stairs rooms, and passed the night in drinking, smoking, and singing,
until they dropped off to sleep in their chairs, or on the floor. An
important fight drew crowds of three or four thousand, and it was
estimated that if the vehicles gathered at any one of them had been
placed in a line they would have reached from Crawley to London.

A favourite diversion of the 'twenties and 'thirties, after the appearance of the steamboat, was the Aquatic Excursion. Sailing vessels
had for many years run to coastal towns near London—among them
the famous Old Margate Hoy—and with the coming of steam the
traffic increased. So many people made their journeys to these
places by water that the coaches found it unprofitable to run to
certain seaside places near the Estuary. Surtees, writing in the early
'thirties, about the traffic on the Dover road, refers to this:

Coaching, however, is but a sorry business on the Dover road just now.
The unequal contest that the proprietors have to maintain with the
steamboats tells sadly against them. From London to Herne Bay a
passenger may be conveyed for half a crown, and for a less sum thence to
Dover by land, whereas formerly it could not be accomplished much
under a pound, going the cheapest way to work. We were credibly
informed at Dover that a coach had made two journeys with only three
passengers; and that, too, in the month of June, a time when many honest
people begin to emigrate to the coast.

All sorts of people began to use the week-end for holiday and relaxation, and on Saturdays the boats from London Bridge to Margate and Ramsgate, and those that made trips round the Nore, were always crowded. On one occasion the passengers on the Margate hoy had a little adventure. The hoy had accidentally had communication with a vessel performing quarantine, and it and all its passengers were detained. A contemporary account says that "the distress of the passengers partook of the serio-comic; at first provisions were very scanty, and they had no prospect but seven weeks of durance. This, to the trippers to the seaside for a week, would have been a serious affair. The vessel, we hear, has since been released."

Dickens described two or three of these Aquatic Excursions in his Boz *Sketches*, and Surtees, in the *New Sporting Magazine*, showed Jorrocks on a week-end trip to Margate. Those who have ever, in the course of studying their average fellow creatures, made a boat trip to Margate in recent years, may compare their own observations with those of Surtees. They will note how little, in a hundred and ten years, the people, the atmosphere, and the proceedings (notably in the matter of food) have changed. Jorrocks boarded the boat with a telescope and a large hamper. His friend the Yorkshireman asked what he had in the hamper. "Why, wittles, to be sure. You seem to forget we are going a woyage, and 'ow keen the sea hair is. I've brought a knuckle of veal, half a ham, beef, sarsingers, chickens, sherry white, and all that sort of thing, and werry acceptable they'll be by the time we get to the Nore." Just as the boat was starting, a young friend of Jorrocks boarded her. He, too, carried food—a baked pigeon and some cold macaroni.

The boat was furnished, as in our own time, with a band for dancing, though its composition was a little different from those of to-day. It was harp, flute, lute, and two horns. It led off with a quadrille, and after the quadrille was done the eating began and went on steadily, with intervals for dancing, till the end of the journey. Jorrocks' return was not so happy. He set off on Sunday afternoon, and as there was no steamer he took the hoy, whose captain guaranteed to land him at Blackwall by ten o'clock. His two friends stayed until Monday morning, when they returned by steamer. Two steamers left Margate each Monday morning at exactly the same hour, and the town crier went round announcing the sailing, at nine o'clock precisely, of the *Magnet* and the *Royal Adelaide*:

> At the end of the jetty, on each side, lay the *Royal Adelaide* and the *Magnet*, with as fierce a contest for patronage as ever was witnessed. Both decks were crowded with anxious faces—for the Monday's steamboat race

69   Omnibuses in the Strand, *ca.* 1850

70   Shillibeer's Omnibus, 1829

71 Knife-board Omnibuses at the Mansion House, *ca.* 1859

is as great an event as a Derby, and a cockney would as lieve lay on an outside horse as patronise a boat that was likely to let another pass her. Nay, so high is the enthusiasm carried that books are regularly made on the occasion, and there is as much clamour for bets as in the ring at Epsom or Newmarket. "Tomkins, I'll lay you a dinner for three, *Royal Adelaide* against the *Magnet*," bawled Jenkins from the former boat. "Done," cries Tomkins. "The *Magnet* for a bottle of port," bawled out another. "A whitebait dinner for two, the *Magnet* reaches Greenwich first." "I'll bet a bottom of brandy on the *Magnet*," roars out the mate.

The two friends took the *Magnet*, which, after a tussle, got ahead of the *Royal Adelaide*. As they approached the mouth of the Medway, they were hailed by a forlorn-looking person seated in the stern of a sailing-vessel. It was Jorrocks in the hoy, which, since three o'clock the previous afternoon, had got just that far.

All through the early years of the century, tentative experiments were being made with steam land-carriages. These afforded excellent material to ribald lampooners and caricaturists. The first essays, made as early as 1781, came to nothing; but from 1800 onwards, machines were produced which did at least "go." During the eighteen-twenties four well-known engineers—Hancock, Gurney, Sir Charles Dance and Ogle—produced steam carriages. The most succsssful was Gurney's, though on its first trial down the Bath Road, a crowd of men hostile to new ideas, especially machinery, attacked it with stones and wrecked it. In the eighteen-thirties a number of steam-traction companies were formed. Hancock ran steam-carriages in London, and though the general feeling was against them—it was held that at any moment the boilers might burst—he had quite a large patronage from the public. And this, in spite of the fact that, in the face of popular apprehension, he named one of them—The Autopsy.

Other ideas for speedier travel were of a rather eccentric kind. One was that of a horseless carriage to which high-flying kites should be attached. It would thus be drawn along by the pull of the kite, but of course was dependent upon the way of the wind. The balloon was also brought into consideration. It was a popular side-show in pleasure-gardens; the prejudice against it had been conquered by free trips, and it was thought that it might be used for regular transport. In 1820 the earliest form of bicycle appeared on the roads— the hobby-horse—a contraption of iron and wood propelled by the rider, who sat astride with toes just touching the ground, and swung his legs back and forth. Its trade name was Pedestrian Curricle It had a short life, and nothing in that form appeared for another forty years, when the velocipede or bone-shaker was put out. But by the early eighteen-thirties all those ideas for speedier travel were extinguished and forgotten in the enthusiasm aroused by the thing that was to ruin coaching, to ruin main-road inns, and to leave the turnpikes for some sixty years to a solitude in which grass grew on ground that had never for more than a few minutes been free of hoofs and wheels. The railway arrived.

72 "Pedestrian Hobby-horse"

73 "The Ladies' Hobby"

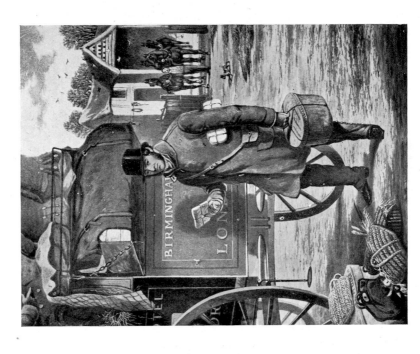

75 "The Guard of 1832"

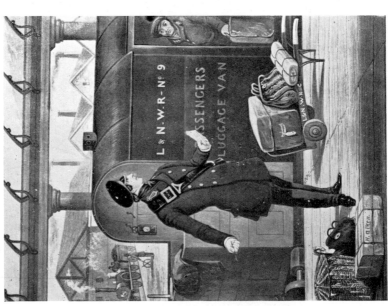

74 "The Guard of 1852"

CHAPTER FIVE
The Age of Steam

THE HOOTS and gibes and execrations with which the middle-aged and elderly greeted the new "tea-kettle" and "potato-can" travel are a familiar feature of our social history. They prophesied this and that about it, and they were very much out in their prophecies. But they were no more out than those of the opposite side; those who not only welcomed the new method, but saw in it the promise of a fair new world. The attitude of the pro-railway group was rather that of our B.B.C. when it launched the radio upon the world, and adopted that motto which now brings a heartache or an acid smile. When every night the world's air throbs with hate, and radio is as potent a weapon of war as the gun, one has to smile, so that one may not weep, when one remembers that it was launched with the motto: "Nation shall speak peace unto Nation."

So those who welcomed the railway saw it as more than a rapid and comfortable means of transit. They actually saw it as a factor in world-peace. They did not foresee the armoured train. They did not foresee that the railway would be just one more means for the rapid movement of aggressive armies. None of them foresaw that the more we are together—the nearer nations are to each other in the means of communication—the more chances there are of war. Any boy or girl who is one of a large family knows that. Yet a poet of the early railway times, Charles Mackay, expressed the opinion of many serious people, in one of the verses of a poem on the New Railway. His sentiments are similar to those which radio at first evoked:

> Lay down your rails, ye nations, near and far;
> Yoke your full trains to Steam's triumphal car;
> Link town to town, and in these iron bands
> Unite the strange and oft-embattled lands.
> Peace and Improvement round each train shall soar,
> And Knowledge light the Ignorance of yore.
> Men, joined in amity, shall wonder long
> That Hate had power to lead their fathers wrong;
> Or that false glory lured their hearts astray,
> And made it virtuous and sublime to slay.
> Blessings on Science and her handmaid Steam
> They make Utopia only half a dream.

In the beginning, those who were against the new thing had quite a body of opinion on their side. It was gathered from the commercial world, the squirearchy, the peerage, the political, economic, and medical world. The medical views were as funny as they always are about anything. Whenever any new invention is put forward, those for it and those against it can always find medical men to approve or condemn. The anti railway group produced doctors who said that tunnels would be most dangerous to public health: they would produce colds, catarrhs and consumptions. The deafening noise, the gloom, the glare of the engine fire, would have a bad effect on the nerves. Further, being moved through the air at a high speed would do grave injury to delicate lungs. In those with high blood-pressure, the movement of the train might produce apoplexy. The sudden plunging of a train into the darkness of a tunnel, and the equally sudden rush into full daylight, would cause great damage to eyesight. But the pro-railway group was of course able to produce equally eminent medical men to say just the opposite. They said that the speed and swing of the train would equalise the circulation, promote digestion, tranquillise the nerves, and ensure good sleep.

The squirearchy hated the thing because it spoiled their "views" and might spoil their sport by running alongside their preserves. "How would any member," a country M.P. cried, "like to have a railroad under his parlour window?" That is why, in some parts of the country, the railway station of a particular town is a mile away from that town; the local landowner wouldn't allow the promoters to acquire rights over his land at any price. One section of the commercial world thought that the thing was unworkable and unsound. Another thought that instead of helping industry it would damage it by concentrating it into a few hands. Some country opponents thought it would have a disastrous effect in frightening animals and birds. One or two cases proved their contention. In 1830, the first railway (the Stockton and Darlington, opened in 1825) was indicted as a nuisance on this very ground. Certain portions of the line ran parallel with the road, and there had been many accidents through horses taking fright, and throwing their riders, or bolting with a gig or phaeton and overturning it. Other opponents were certain economists, as unreliable then as they are now. They held that the railway could not possibly "pay." There would not be a sufficiently large number of people willing to face the risk of such a mode of travel.

In the event, of course, the railway conquered all opposition, and

soon there was no doubt as to whether it would "pay." During the
'thirties and 'forties there was the same scramble to get "in" railways
as we have seen later with other new and popular projects, and plans
for new lines and new companies were issued by the score. But
early railway travel cannot have been very pleasant. On some lines
the coach was brought in as collaborator. Thus if, in 1838, you
wanted to go from London to Birmingham, you had to break the
journey at one point, and take a coach. "Peter Pry," writing in the
New Sporting Magazine, shows that you went by train from Euston
to Denbigh Hall, where the order was "All Change." On leaving
the platform and descending the stairs to the yard:

> I . . . was stopped by a check-taker, just as though it were a theatre,
> who, after taking my ticket, and looking at the tickets of those who were
> booked through to Birmingham, to whom he gave large pink cards with
> the numbers of the coaches that were to convey them, and other particu-
> lars inscribed thereon . . . we descended the long flight of steps, and a
> sudden turn disclosed a score of coaches and omnibuses all standing under a
> covered building alongside of a turnpike road below, with post-boys and
> horses for carriages, porters to carry the luggage, policemen, inspectors,
> all waiting to forward the passengers to Birmingham.

The writer, who had booked only to Denbigh Hall, took a ticket to
Birmingham, and was driven by coach to Rugby station, where they
alighted and were taken on to Birmingham by train. He adds that
at every turn the traveller found himself requested to abstain from
all gratuities to railway servants.

The actual rolling-stock was, in its appointments, anything but
comfortable. If it was a test of endurance to sit for four hours outside a coach in rain, or inside in fug, the railway offered little more in
the way of comfort. Certainly the first-class carriages had cushioned
seats; but the second-class had only narrow bare boards, while the
third-class had nothing at all; no seats and no roof; they were just
open trucks. So that third-class passengers gained nothing from the
new mode except speed. In the matter of comfort, indeed, they
lost; they did, on the coaches, have a seat, but now they had to stand
all the way, which gave opportunities to the comic press. This kind
of thing: "A man was seen yesterday buying a third-class ticket for
the new London and Birmingham Railway. The state of his mind
is being enquired into."

A writer in the early days of railways wrote feelingly of both
second- and third-class carriages. He made the suggestion that the
directors of the railways must have sent all over the world to find the
hardest possible wood. Of the open third-class trucks he said that

they had the peculiar property of meeting the rain from whatever quarter it came. He described them as horizontal shower-baths, from whose searching power there was no escape. A wet, steaming, dripping coach was, he said, a melancholy enough object, but it was nothing to the third-class trucks in wet weather. To escape the rain was impossible. If the traveller turned his back to it, it went down his collar. If he faced it, his pockets became wells. If he took it sideways, his ears were filled with it. Yet in spite of these discomforts, one of the earliest passenger-carrying railways, the Liverpool and Manchester, in its first year (1830) carried 445,000 passengers. Objections continued, but nothing could prevail against the fact that one train could carry as many people as thirty mail-coaches, and a far greater bulk of goods than a hundred coaches.

A large section went on bewailing the passing of the coach, and pointing out the miseries of rail-travel and the ugliness the railways had brought to the countryside. The coachmen, of course, and their laureates in prose and verse, were particularly vocal. There is the well-known *Lamentation of the Knights of the Whip*:

> Ah, the good days of coaching are past like a dream,
> And we, the Crack Dragsmen, are victims to steam;
> There are many good fellows have cause to bewail
> The old line of Road and the new line of Rail. . . .
> And won't our good Queen do a something for us?
> Or must we be doomed to a Company's bus?
> O Steam, thou art nought but the waggoners' curse.
> Now hear all the changes, can any be worse?
> For the tapering crop you now witness a poker,
> For the spruce turned-out coachman a smutty-faced stoker. . . .
> For the neat roadside inn and a dish of cold meat
> You've a gorgeous saloon, but there's no time to eat.
> O Vulcans! O Drivers! with Tartarean faces,
> Can you ever expect to win our good graces?
> An emblem of hell are your factory stations,
> Exciting our pity, or vile execrations.

Among the objectors were Wordsworth and De Quincey. When a railway through the Lakes was proposed, Wordsworth lavished a protesting sonnet on the project, in which he asked:

> Is there no nook of English ground secure
> From rash assault? Schemes of retirement sown
> In youth, and 'mid the busy world kept pure
> As when their earliest flowers of hope were blown,
> Must perish; how can they this blight endure?
> And must he too his old delights disown,
> Who scorns a false utilitarian lure
> 'Mid his paternal fields at random thrown. . . .

And so on, ending with an appeal to the passing winds and torrents to speak against the wrong. De Quincey's objection to the thing was that it robbed the traveller of what he considered one of the delights of road-travel—the *sense* of speed:

> They boast of more velocity, not, however, as a consciousness but as a fact of our lifeless knowledge, resting upon alien evidence; as, for instance, because somebody *says* that we have gone fifty miles in the hour, though we are far from feeling it as a personal experience; or upon the evidence of a result, as that actually we find ourselves in York four hours after leaving London. . . . But, seated on the old mail-coach we needed no evidence out of ourselves to indicate the velocity. . . . The vital experience of the glad animal sensibilities made doubt impossible on the question of our speed; we heard our speed, we saw it, we felt it, as a thrilling; and this speed was not the product of blind insensate agencies, that had no sympathy to give, but was incarnated in the fiery eyeballs of the noblest among brutes, in his dilated nostril, spasmodic muscles, and thunder-beating hoofs.
>
> But now, on the new system of travelling, iron tubes and boilers have disconnected man's heart from the ministers of his locomotion. . . . Tidings, fitted to convulse all nations, must henceforward travel by culinary process; and the trumpet that once announced from afar the laurelled mail, heart-shaking when heard screaming on the wind and proclaiming itself through the darkness to every village or solitary house on its route, has now given way for ever to the pot-wallopings of the boiler.

A writer named "Phœnix" wrote in 1838 in a similar strain:

> A railway conveyance is a locomotive prison. At a certain period you are compelled to place your person and property in the custody of a set of men exceedingly independent, and who have little regard for your accommodation. Till your journey is accomplished, you are completely subservient to their commands. You pass through the country without much opportunity of contemplating its beauties; you are subjected to the monotonous clatter of its machinery, and every now and then to the unpleasant grating sensation of the brake. To all these things must be added the horribly offensive smells of rancid oil and smoky coal.

The railway enthusiasts retorted by pointing to the miseries of coach travel and its snail's pace. They reminded the public that with railway travel there was none of the distress of finding "no room," and having to wait till next day; there were no surly guards and coachmen demanding tips at every ten miles; no clambering over dirty wheels; no being wedged among piles of dusty luggage; no plying of the whip on tired animals. They reiterated the advantages of speedy travel. They referred to the number of people, even well-to-do squires who, in the pre-railway days, never crossed the border of the county in which they were born, and knew no more of the general features of their own country than of the moon. The spread of ideas, they cried, as well as the conveyance of persons and merchandise, depended greatly on means of transit; men could become better acquainted with the conditions and habits of their fellow men, and ignorance would diminish before the onward and resistless march of knowledge and of truth. Never before, they went on, could travelling be enjoyed at so little trouble and expense, and in proof that the new invention had firmly established itself, they pointed to the vast business being done in carpet-bags, trunks and portmanteaux, wrappers, caps, cushions, rugs, and Railway Guides.

But with all its triumphs, the railway seemed to lack something. Its enthusiasts wrote a great deal about it, but none of them caught the glowing, fervid note of the coaching writers. Certainly its appointments did not afford much scope for lyricism. The whole subject was clouded in smoke and smut. The earliest stations were little more than sheds, against which the façade of our King's Cross station is almost beautiful. The convenience was no real advance on the coach discomfort. The railway was perhaps a blessing, but nobody was inspired by it. With few exceptions, they wrote in plain, jog-trot, Podsnappian approval of something useful.

One of the enthusiasts lets his subject badly down when he comes to the refreshment departments of those early lines. He speaks of Wolverton as being remarkable in having an extremely handsome refreshment room. But it seems to have learned something from the tricks of the coach dinner, since it was chiefly remarkable for its scalding-hot coffee, which had to be drunk in five minutes. When the traveller asked for some milk to cool it, he was always given boiling milk. At another station where the usual five-minute stop for refreshments was made, the writer was one of many who had just secured a cup of coffee, when the bell rang, and the call came: "Take your seats, please!" They left their coffee, and dashed to the train, and the train stood for another three minutes. Before it left, they saw their full cups of coffee emptied back into the urn for the next train.

The hot soup of Swindon was as famous as the scalding coffee of Wolverton. And with all his enthusiasm for the Swindon refreshment room, the writer cannot meet the coach enthusiasts on their own ground when he comes to the refreshments they served—sandwiches, sausage-rolls, sherry and biscuit, veal-pie and porter. Bad as some of the coach dinners were, the railway food marked a sad decline from what was provided at the average coaching-inn. And still does to-day; the dining-car meal can seldom be favourably compared with that of an equivalent restaurant and price. Dickens, a stern critic of public institutions, whether of the coaching age (as in his pictures of the White Horse of Ipswich and the Golden Cross of London) or of the railway age, had a good deal to say on railway refreshment rooms and railway hotels. Here is one of his flicks:

What with skimming over the open landscape, what with mining in the damp bowels of the earth, what with banging, booming, and shrieking the scores of miles away, I am hungry when I arrive at the "refreshment" station where I am expected. Please to observe—expected. . . . The apartment that is to restore me is a wind-trap cunningly set to inveigle all the draughts in that countryside, and to communicate a special intensity to them as they rotate in two hurricanes; one about my wretched head, one about my wretched legs. The training of the young ladies behind the counter has been directed on the assumption of a defiant dramatic show that I am *not* expected. . . . Chilling fast, and subdued by the moral disadvantage at which I stand, I turn my disconsolate eyes on the refreshments that are to restore me. I find that I must either scald my throat by insanely ladling into it, against time and for no wager, brown hot water stiffened with flour; or I must make myself flaky and sick with Banbury cake; or I must stuff into my delicate organisation a currant pincushion which I know will swell.

In a later passage he describes the terminus restaurants as no better. He pictures himself as reaching the station in time to dine before boarding the train. But—"I cannot dine on stale sponge cakes. I cannot dine on shining brown patties composed of unknown animals within, and offering to my view the device of an indigestible star-fish in leaden pie-crust. I cannot dine on a sandwich. I cannot dine on barley-sugar. I cannot dine on toffee." His views of the Railway Hotel are not much more pleasant. "We all know," he says, "the new hotel near the railway station, where it is always gusty, in the lane which is always muddy." He then, contradicting his statement that everybody knows it, proceeds to describe it. He describes the flooring of the passages that is too new, and the walls that are too new, and the gritty feeling of mortar. He describes the cracked doors and the warped shutters. He describes the very new people who have come to keep the very new hotel, and the very new furniture which won't settle down and is always in the wrong places. He describes the maps of damp on the walls. He describes the mortar in the sandwich, the mortar in the sherry, the mortar in the bedroom chimney which prevents the smoke from rising. He describes the general *greenness* of the whole establishment, and the sense that business is being done on wholesale lines, so that nobody is glad to see the traveller, or sorry to see him, or cares whether he comes or goes, or how he comes or goes; and contrasts this spirit with that of the old inn where one's retail interest in oneself was satisfied.

But with the spread of railway travel, and the death of the road, the old inns were at their last gasp. Many of the lines ran to towns that were off the main road, and brought prosperity to them; while some highway towns, once in the full stream of prosperity, were by-passed and fell to ruin. Midway villages that had done well in the coaching era went into a slumber that lasted some fifty years, and quite large towns were left without any public means of communication, neither railway nor coach. A few old die-hards, in defiance of the spirit of the age, continued to travel by road, and to lend it a little wan life, but generally there was nothing on the road but the carrier's cart and the waggon, which were to be seen up to the 'eighties. They patronised only the ale-houses or minor inns.

The great inns, many of which were actually mansions, had to retire into private life. Some of them tried to struggle on by serving bagmen, as commercial travellers were called, and by serving an occasional hunt-supper and ball; but even so, two-thirds of the house was shut up. Birch-Reynardson, in his *Down the Road*, spoke of their forlorn state and their heavy fall from grandeur to shabbiness— "the great rambling, half-aired, half-appointed inn; waiter acting boots, boots acting post-boy, or maybe all three; and cook acting chambermaid, barmaid, and all." The only thing he regretted, in connection with the coming of the railway, was the extinction of the old posting-inn.

The mail coaches had been taken off the road, and the mails given to railways, by 1841. Most of the stage-coaches had been withdrawn by 1842, and by 1847 everything, including the new steam-coaches, was off, and, as a contemporary said, "the great roads of former days are overgrown with weeds, the coaches broken up or perhaps turned into hen-roosts, and the tea-kettle with its unmelodious whistle has taken full possession of everything and everybody." Among the famous inns that had to close their doors, or close the bulk of their premises, were the Swan, at Tetsworth; the inn at Chapel House, where Johnson spoke his famous piece; the Swan, at Ferrybridge; the Castle, at Marlborough, now part of the college; the Pelican, at Speenhamland; the Bell, at Barnby Moor; the George, at Little Brickhill, on the Holyhead Road; the Lion, at Dunchurch; the inn at Hartford Bridge, on the Exeter road; the Beckhampton Inn, on

76 "Steamed Out: or the starving Stage-Coachman and Boys"

From an engraving by George Cruickshank

77 The Last of a Stage-Coach

From a drawing of ca. 1850

78   First Class

79   Second Class

Both from prints of ca. 1860

the Bath road; and a number of smaller places. Many of these, with the coming of the car, reopened and are now flourishing.

Some of the larger sort were taken over as private houses or hunting-lodges. They were fortunate. Those that lingered on, half-open and half-shut, with their kitchens serving only chops, steaks, and cheese, presented a sad enough spectacle, and one can understand the middle-aged becoming sentimental and grieved. Dickens made a vivid sketch of one of them, which he called the Dodo:

> If the Dodo were only a gregarious bird—if he had only some confused idea of making a comfortable nest—I could hope to get through the hours between this and bed-time, without being consumed by devouring melancholy. But the Dodo's habits are all wrong. It provides me with a trackless desert of sitting-room, with a chair for every day in the year, a table for every month, and a waste of sideboard where a lonely China vase pines in a corner for its mate long departed, and will never make a match with the candlestick in the opposite corner. The Dodo has nothing in the larder. Even now, I behold the Boots returning with my sole in a piece of paper. . . . The Dodo excludes the outer air. When I mount up to my bedroom, a smell of closeness and flue gets lazily up my nose like sleepy snuff. The loose little bits of carpet writhe under my tread, and take wormy shapes. I don't know the ridiculous man in the looking-glass, beyond having met him once or twice in a dish-cover. The Dodo is narrow-minded as to towels; expects me to wash on a freemason's apron without the trimming; when I asked for soap, gives me a stony-hearted something white, with no more lather in it than the Elgin marbles. The Dodo has seen better days, and possesses interminable stables at the back —silent, grass-grown, broken-windowed, horseless.

While the eighteen-thirties had thus revolutionised English travel, the first year of the next decade brought forward a man who was to take a large part in not only English travel but world travel. In 1841 a small and scarcely noted event took place in a provincial town; an event that held the germ of a great international service. The railway by that time had reached Leicester, and a Leicester man named Thomas Cook conceived the idea of doing a service to those unaccustomed to railway travel, and making a little profit for himself. In July of 1841 Thomas Cook carried out his first Conducted Tour. The journey was from Leicester to Loughborough; about eleven miles. The price was one shilling. He collected a party of over six hundred.

But though the railway mania—or rather, the fortune-hunting mania—spread and spread in such a fashion that it looked as if no field of all England would remain unfouled, there were a few minds

o

working on other means.   The balloon had shown the possibilities of
air-travel, and experiments were being made in steerable flying-
machines.   In the early 'forties, many actual flights were made
some around London, and some in other parts.   John Ashton, in
his volume of Victorian gossip, mentions that in 1842 a Samuel
Henson took out a patent for an apparatus and machinery "for
conveying letters, goods and passengers from place to place through
the air."   He also quotes an account of a flight made by another
aeronaut in 1843.   This pioneer, a Professor Geolls, in a steam-
driven machine, rose to a height of three miles.   Then he crashed.
He was at the time over the sea, and this was his own account of the
crash.

I passed many ships, and in particular one steamer, whose paltry speed,
in comparison with mine, was nothing.   Alas, however, that was not
destined to last, for, just as I had shot ahead of the steamer, something
went wrong with the machinery, and the fanners stopped.   This did not
at all alarm me; for, as described by Mr. Henson, these fanners are only
necessary for propulsion, and not at all requisite for maintaining the
machine in the air.   Unfortunately, however, I forgot in the hurry of the
moment, to remove the weights from the safety-valve, and the effects from
this were disastrous in the extreme.   The great accumulation of steam that
took place was too much for the pipes; and consequently, bang went three
of them, at the same instant.

The machine, at this exact moment, feeling its equilibrium altered,
surged considerably, and the remaining pipes necessarily followed the
example of the others: fizz-bizz-whizz, away they went, one after the
other, like pop-guns.   Unfortunately, one of these pipes, in flying off,
struck a bamboo stretcher, and shattered it so, that the machine, losing
bearance on one side, toppled over and became perfectly unmanageable;
she, in fact, whirled over and over in a way that may be imagined but
which it is altogether impossible to describe.

I, of course, was now descending with fearful rapidity, and nothing was
left me to contemplate but death and destruction.   I can only compare
my sensations at this moment to those experienced in a nightmare.
Sensibility now forsook me; and indeed this was not to be wondered at, in
consequence of the whirling of the machine.   On coming to my senses
again, I found myself in bed, with severe headache, nausea and vomiting,
the usual accompaniments of such a flight through the air.

The despised steamer had seen his descent, and had launched a
boat to pick him up.   The machine was a total loss.   After his
recovery, he announced his willingness to try again.

But in the thick of all those new improvements of railways and
steamers, came a sudden scare which suggested that they would all

prove futile. There was another earthquake scare; a prophecy that on a certain date the whole of London was to be engulfed. In March of 1842, as in March of 1750, there was a panic flight. All the timid, both rich and poor, bolted like rabbits. The roads were again crowded; also the railway and the steamers. Some business men, blindly accepting the prophecy, sold their businesses for instant cash, and got away. Men with salaried posts resigned their posts. The well-to-do set out in their carriages and chaises, and, as in our own time, Brighton was their city of refuge. The earthquake was timed for March 16th, and a Brighton paper pilloried the large number of families of the middle and upper classes who had filled the town during the two preceding days. On the night of the 15th, twenty carriages arrived there—a phenomenon that had not been seen since the opening of the London and Brighton Railway.

John Ashton, in the book already mentioned, quotes from the *Times* of March 17th:

The scene witnessed in the neighbourhoods of St. Giles and Seven Dials during the whole of yesterday was perhaps the most singular that has presented itself for many years. Many of the Irish resident in those localities have left for the shore of the Emerald Isle, but by far the larger number, unblessed with this world's goods, have been compelled to remain where they are, and to anticipate the fearful event which was to engulf them in the bowels of the earth. . . . The poor Irish, however, are not the only persons who have been credulous in this matter; many persons from whom better things might have been expected were amongst the number who left London. To the Gravesend steamboat companies the "earthquake" proved a source of immense gain; and the same may be said with regard to the different railways. . . . About 11 o'clock the *Planet* came alongside the London Bridge Wharf, and the rush to get on board of her was tremendous, and, in a few minutes, there was scarcely standing room on board. The trains on the various railways were, during the whole of Tuesday and yesterday morning, unusually busy in conveying passengers without the proscribed limits of the metropolitan disaster. . . . On the north, Hampstead and Highgate were favoured with a visit from larger bodies of the respectable inhabitants of St. Giles; and Primrose Hill also was selected as a famous spot for viewing the demolition of the leviathan city. The darkness of the day, and the thickness of the atmosphere, however, prevented it being seen.

Under the triumph of the railway the roads, of course, being little used, received no attention; which made things very irksome for the few who still had to use them. The turnpikes, as Surtees said, were altogether neglected, save in the matter of the officers' sinecure salaries; and the nearer a turnpike was to a railway, the worse it was. In one of his novels he presents a character making a night-drive by dog-cart across country, and missing the way, and finding broken signposts with obliterated letters, foul roads, and no traffic on them from which he could get a direction. By the 'sixties, many of the roads had sunk back to their Queen Anne state. In the 'twenties a number of new coach roads had been begun, but with the coming of the railway they were abandoned and left half-made. Silence and desolation haunted the highways that a while ago had rung with incessant business. A rot set in, and they sank back into the twilight from which they had, only five centuries earlier, emerged. Surfaces became pudding, eighteen inches deep. Hedges thrust themselves over the ditches. The branches of untended trees formed an arch over the road. Some of the great highways became grass-tracks. It seemed to everybody that never again would the road be wanted.

Yet with all the enthusiasm which the railway aroused, few people wrote any account of their railway travels. The many records of travel by road, some of which have been quoted earlier, are in no way matched by records of the rail. This is not surprising. There was so little to say. They got into the train. At Wolverton they got out of the train, and ate a pork-pie. They returned to the train, and arrived at Birmingham in the time their fathers had taken to reach Stony Stratford. That was all. The journey was undertaken and accomplished. Its detail and incident never reached the traveller. When a coach stopped, the passengers knew why it had stopped. When a train stopped, nobody except the unapproachable driver knew why. Nobody could see what was ahead of them or behind them. All the minutiæ of progress, of which, as De Quincey said, the coach traveller was fully aware, were, in the new thing, lost.

Hawthorne, during his consulship in England (1853-7) made many little tours of our island, and left, in *Our Old Home*, some charming but quite clear-sighted impressions of us and our institutions. He found little pleasure in his railway travels:

On a railway, I suspect, what little we do see of the country is seen quite amiss, because it was never intended to be looked at from any point of view in that straight line; so that it is like looking at the wrong side of a piece of tapestry. The old highways and footpaths were as natural as brooks and rivulets, and adapted themselves by an inevitable impulse to the physiognomy of the country; and, furthermore, every object within view of them had some subtle reference to their curves and undulations; but the line of a railway is perfectly artificial, and puts all precedent things at sixes-and-sevens. At any rate, be the cause what it may, there is seldom anything worth seeing within the scope of a railway traveller's eye; and if there were, it requires an alert marksman to take a flying shot at the picturesque. . . .

The railway was exciting, but it was not in itself a pleasure. Nobody went up and down the line, day by day for two or three weeks, for joy of going up and down. A few student engineers perhaps made repeated journeys for the purpose of comparing the performances of the different lines; but that was rather business interest than pleasure. I can find no accounts of Six Weeks' Tour through the English Counties by Railway. Things of that kind have been done in our own time, as a part of railway advertising but I know of nothing done in the early days. The railway writing of those days concerned itself solely with the marvel of speed. We of to-day accepted air-travel quite casually. The news that we could reach Paris in two hours instead of seven caused no excitement. But well into the 'seventies, writers were still stressing the wonder of getting from London to York in a few hours. Long before Kipling felt it necessary to acclaim the railway:

> "Romance is dead." . . . And all unseen,
> Romance brought up the nine-fifteen. . . .

long before that, in the middle of the century, poets wrote songs to the railway, though, as I said earlier, their subject never inspired them. They did this kind of thing:

> A mile a minute—on we go!
> Hurrah! my courser fast.
> With coal-black mane and fiery train
> Through winter's storm and blast.

And this:

> The earth has a thousand noble things that loud for praises call,
> But the grimy engine black with smoke is as noble as them all.

And Walter Thornbury, in a volume of sketches, wrote on *The Poetry of Railways*. But always with an emphasis on speed:

> Men see no poetry in being shot as from a cannon, or passing from Bath to Bristol with the speed of a planet on a tour, or a fallen star bent on pleasure. . . . Know, O insensate man, that that sound of the engine is like the champ and tramp of a thousand horse: it might be Tamerlane riding to conquest: it might be Alaric thundering at the gates of Rome. . . . We are gliding on golden rails that the sunset shines on, and we are just about to thread an arch. When we lean back, and the great smoke-clouds that roll around us grow crimson in the sunlight, we shall seem as

if we were in the aerial car of the Indian mythology.   Like a white banner
flies the engine's smoke—and away it rolls—stooping to join the great
white fog that has no wings, and sits and broods yonder about the damp
autumn fields.   Through dark caves of tunnels—through dull barrennesses
of high and bare embankments we rush with the force of a steam-catapult
or a huge case-shot that is never spent—like a battering-ram—in a long
race, for this steam-horse, with fire for blood, never wearies.   Swift round
curves, and swift up low hills—swift past village church and park and
farm-house and wood—over river—along moor—past fat and lean, rich
and poor, rock and clay, meadow and street; for this mad horse never
wearies.

In a later passage he deplores the probability that in another
generation the wonder will have passed.   That the sight of a train
growing out of a cloud of smoke, the terror of its march, and the
battling of its rush, will have grown as commonplace as the horse-bus.
That people will no longer think of the comet speed, of the contrast
of such spiritual power being controlled by a grimy driver, Caliban
controlling Ariel.   They will take it all for granted; as, of course,
they did.   But they never took coaching for granted.

Up to quite a late period of the century, the early discomforts of
railway travel persisted, and complaint brought little improvement.
There seems to have been no proper heating, and the doors of the
carriages must have fitted rather badly, since an essential item of
luggage was the travelling-rug.   One never sees them in use to-day,
but even in the 'eighties travellers carried them to wrap round the
knees and legs.   On the outside of a coach, in nights of winter, rugs
and mufflers can be understood.   Since they were equally necessary
in the railway carriage, then it must have been rather more chilly
with draughts than a box-seat in an open gale.   Second- and third-
class passengers carried cushions as well as rugs.   An American who
visited England in mid-Victorian times compares our trains unfavour-
ably with those of America.   In *The Old Country*, he writes:

> The first-class carriage is truly luxurious, light and splendid with plate-
> glass sides, and furnished with capacious springy seats, and with every
> accommodation for the bestowing of bundles, hats, and umbrellas.   The
> second-class carriage forms a lamentable contrast to this; it is as hard,
> bare, and uncomely a box as oak boards can make it; its seats are un-
> cushioned, and frequently dirtied by the baskets and boots of railway
> workmen and market men.   There seems to be little or no distinction
> between the second- and third-class carriages excepting in this, that the
> second-class carriages are resorted to by the most respectable people, on
> account of the expensiveness of the first.

He has a good word to say for the English railway porter of that time, a time when tips were still forbidden. He says that they expect no fee for their services, but "I was always tempted to break the strict letter of the law, and to reward these men."

Another discomfort of railway travel was the narrow carriages. They gave no room for the stretching of the legs. If the carriage was not full, those on either side could stretch their legs sideways; but in a full carriage one had to sit in stiffness, or, by mutual consent, stretch the legs in between the legs of the man opposite, under what was called "a treaty of legs." Another discomfort was the small number of trains. Unfamiliarity with rail travel often led people to miss their train at a junction, and let themselves in for a long wait. Sometimes the train, after lingering so long at a station that the passengers got out for a "stretch," would go off without warning, and those left behind would learn that the next train was due in five hours.

Surtees, in 1851, published a small volume for the benefit of the inexperienced—*Hints to Railway Travellers*. He tells them how to deal with their luggage. If they are going to London for a stay of some weeks, they should pack it into one large crate and send it in advance by goods train. If they take it with them, he advises them to have plenty of luggage labels, either of leather or parchment. Travellers in those days seem to have taken half the house with them, since he advises them to number their boxes and packages from 1 to 40, and to keep a list of the contents of each package from 1 to 40. He also gives them advice how to comport themselves at the departure station:

Let someone keep a sharp look-out on your luggage while you take the tickets; carry the tickets of the whole party in your glove or waistcoat pocket, to be ready to show whenever they are asked for. Always anticipate an asking. Hold the tickets like a hand at cards, so that they may easily be counted. When the train comes you must take such seats as are vacant when it arrives, unless you have interest with the station-master to secure you a carriage from the starting-place, or have one ready to attach when the train arrives. A glove, or book, or anything left on a seat denotes that it is taken. Take yours that way.

See your luggage put on the roof of the carriage you occupy, and book the number of the carriage (which is often in a very indistinct place about the wheels), or you may have difficulty in finding it if you get out of the train after it is lengthened.

He advises them to carry their own provisions, so that they may dine when they are hungry instead of when the railway directors think they should be.   He suggests that they should have a newspaper as a protection against the people who will talk.   If they buy the *Times* at starting, they can exchange it at the first stop for the *Post*, and at the next stop they can exchange the *Post* for the *Chronicle*. He speaks somewhat acidly of the London hotels, as good places to keep out of, and recommends lodgings.   It may surprise readers of to-day to learn that "the streets in the vicinity of St. James's Street and Pall Mall are full of bedroom lodgings where gentlemen get capitally put up for 2*s*. or 3*s*. a night."   He advises visitors from the country not to travel with their own servants:

> They are of no use in London.   If you do not lose them in going up you are sure to do so when you get there; besides which they generally think they are brought for their own amusement and not for your service. Moreover, they learn no good in London lodgings.

The index of each volume of the *Annual Register* for the 'fifties, 'sixties and 'seventies, contains, under Railway Accidents, a string of entries.   Notable accidents were that at Staplehurst in 1865, when part of a train crashed over a viaduct, and the rest hung suspended; and that on the Tay Bridge in 1879.   The Tay Bridge disaster happened on a wild night of December.   The train from Edinburgh to Dundee was crossing its two-mile length when part of it collapsed, and fell, with the whole train, into the sea.   All the passengers, 70 in number, the driver, the stoker and the guard, were drowned.   When divers went down, not a single body could be found in the carriages or among the broken girders.   Only after some days were a few brought up.   The actual cause of the accident was never discovered —whether the train had been blown over in the gale, and thus smashed the bridge, or whether the bridge had been carried away before the train reached it.   There was no witness to say one word.

The Staplehurst disaster was not so dreadful, but it caused the death of ten people, and serious injury to twenty.   It is remembered to-day for the miraculous escape of one of its passengers, who was in one of the suspended carriages, and for the coincidence (to him) of its date.   It happened on June 9th, the very date on which, five years later, he died.   He had with him the manuscript of two numbers of *Our Mutual Friend*, on which he was then engaged, and after he had done what he could in helping the injured, his first thought was for his manuscript.   Writing to Forster the next day, he said:

> I was in the terrific Staplehurst accident yesterday, and worked for hours among the dying and the dead.   I was in the carriage that did not

80 An Early "Flyer" arriving at a Station

81 "The Fearful Accident on the North London Railway at Kentish Town Fields, September 2nd, 1861"

82 The Railway Station (1862)
From the painting by W. P. Frith

go over, but went off the line, and hung over the bridge in an inexplicable manner. No words can describe the scene.

In a Postscript to the last number of that novel, he gave the public a lighter description:

On Friday the ninth of June in the present year Mr. and Mrs. Boffin (in their manuscript dress of receiving Mr. and Mrs. Lammle at breakfast) were on the South Eastern Railway with me, in a terribly destructive accident. When I had done what I could to help others, I climbed back into my carriage—nearly turned over a viaduct, and caught aslant upon the turn—to extricate the worthy couple. They were much soiled, but otherwise unhurt. The same happy result attended Miss Bella Wilfer on her wedding-day, and Mr. Riderhood inspecting Bradley Headstone's red neckerchief as he lay asleep. I remember with devout thankfulness that I can never be much nearer parting company with my readers for ever, than I was then.

While the railway has developed in the direction of comfort and safety, it has developed but little in speed. It reached a certain point and there stopped, as most mechanical devices do. Quite early in its history its engines could do sixty miles an hour, and sometimes short bursts beyond that speed. Its "times" to-day are still much what they were seventy years ago. To-day you can go from London to York in four hours. So you could in 1855. The journey to Paris in the 'seventies took seven hours. It still does; or did, up to September 1939.

Real comfort was long in coming. In 1850, the railway supplied special carriages for invalids who had to travel, but not much attention was paid to the ordinary traveller. Our railways had had over forty years of life, forty years of the boiling soup of Swindon and the scalding coffee of Wolverton, before the dining-car and the sleeping-car were introduced. They were introduced in 1873 as the result of a casual visit to America by the then chairman of the Midland line. He found them everywhere in America on long-distance routes, and as he found them most convenient, he made arrangements for the use of George Pullman's cars on his own line. The example was quickly followed by the South Eastern and the Great Western, and it spread to the other lines. But nearly another twenty years were to pass before the corridor train appeared. This was first used by the South Eastern in 1892. Foot-warmers for the carriages had been introduced in the late 'seventies, and that was the only warmth the passengers were given until 1893, when hot-water pipes were run under the floors of the carriages.

P

In the 'fifties and 'sixties, travelling on foot ceased to be a social degradation. The walking-tour became popular. It was not then called hiking, and it never should have been. Hiking suggests a strenuous covering of ground; what they did in the middle of the century was the more leisurely stroll. Some of those foot travellers left accounts of their tours, and they make pleasant, quiet reading in these times. The few accounts one has seen of hiking have something of crowd and clamour about them; they do not convey the spirit of the true walking-tour, the spirit of solitude and calm which arises from the books of that time.

One of them, *A Londoner's Walk to the Land's End*, by Walter White, describes a tour from Southampton through Dorset, Devon, and Cornwall, in the course of which he walked four hundred and twenty-five miles. It cost him, including a trip to the Scilly Isles, ten pounds. Unlike the foot travellers of the coaching days, he was nowhere refused a bed because he was a pedestrian. When he did meet a refusal, the reason was that the landlady hadn't the accommodation for making a guest "real comfortable." At all inns, and at town hotels, he was accepted without question. Similar books, which came about the same time, are Walter Thornbury's *Cross Country;* and *Rambles*, by William Allingham, the Irish poet, issued under the pseudonym "Patricius Walker."

Another tour was that fortnight's wandering through Cumberland and Yorkshire by Dickens and Wilkie Collins, described in *The Lazy Tour of Two Idle Apprentices.* Writing to Forster in 1856, Dickens announced that he and Collins were going off on an expedition to out-of-the-way places, avoiding railways, and nosing out old inns. They fixed on the fells of Cumberland, and started from Carlisle. They discovered several old inns, sketches of which are given in the narrative, and among other exploits they climbed Carrick Fell where, on the summit, they were lost in rain and darkness. In scrambling down (a journey of two hours), Wilkie Collins fell and sprained his ankle. Dickens and the landlord of their inn, who had acted as guide, had to carry him down:

> We got down at last in the wildest place, preposterously out of the course; and, propping up C. against stones, sent Mr. P. to the other side of Cumberland for dog-cart, so got back to his inn, and changed. Shoe or stocking on the bad foot out of the question. Foot bundled up in a flannel waistcoat. C. D. carrying C. melodramatically (Wardour to the life!) everywhere; into and out of carriages; up and down stairs; to bed; every step. And so to Wigton, got doctor, and here we are!

He found Wigton a town of little houses in half-mourning, white

stone and black; and noted that though it seemed to have no popula-
tion, no business, and no streets to speak of, they could see within
range of their inn window five linen-drapers, and found another
next door, and five more round the corner. They ended the tour at
Doncaster in St. Leger week, and found the crowd of sporting men
"a gathering of vagabonds from all parts of the racing earth."

Most of the tours made at that time were by lane and footpath
and bridle-path. The main roads in most parts of the country were
still asleep. Even the drovers and the carriers' carts used the by-roads
in order to avoid the toll-gates. Why these gates survived, when
their revenues must have been so small, is a mystery, but in the
'sixties there were still nearly five thousand toll-gate keepers. Some
of the gates were abolished in the late 'seventies, but others survived
into the 'nineties. Possibly the reason for keeping them on was to
provide jobs for old pensioners who were useless for anything else.
As Tony Weller said: "They're all on 'em men as has met with some
disappointments in life. . . . Consequence of vich, they retires from
the world, and shuts themselves up in pikes; partly with the view of
being solitary, and partly to rewenge themselves on mankind by
taking tolls." In the mid-Victorian days, though they lived on the
Queen's Highway, they lived as retired a life as they could have
found in any remote hamlet, with perhaps only three chances a day
of "rewenge."

But here and there, in far-away corners, a few minor roads still
saw a little life. While the railway had spread its "grid-iron" over
almost all the fields of England, there were odd spaces which it had
not covered, and in those spaces local journeys were made by the
elsewhere-forgotten coach. Cornwall, for example, was one of the
last places to receive a railway service, and the coach was seen there,
on by-roads, in a generation which, in other parts, had always done
its travel by rail. Some of the coaches used in Cornwall and Cumberland and parts of Yorkshire were the very coaches which had been
celebrated by writers and artists when they were making records on
the great turnpikes—the Brighton Road, the Great North Road,
the Shrewsbury and Holyhead Road, the Bath Road. This was their
sunset, this local jobbing along the subsidiary roads, carrying people
to and from market, or helping walking-tourists over the dull patches;
until at last, in a field adjoining some inn, they came to firewood.

Captain Malet, writing in the 'seventies, describes another fate
reserved for them:

Travelling on the Great North Road lately, I asked the owner of a house
which had been a well-known inn but is now a school, if he knew what

had become of the numerous post-chaises. He said there had been one in the yard until lately, and that he had given it to a carpenter in exchange for forms for his schoolboys to sit on. I have seen a number of these yellow po-chays in a carpenter's yard at Cambridge. I have also seen them serving as summer-houses in the gardens attached to neat suburban villas.

In a few other corners not served by rail, the road saw a little life. In some districts a large tract had railway all round it but nothing across it, and there was no way to its interior except by road. Hawthorne records a road journey from Oxford to Woodstock and Blenheim:

> On a fine morning in September, we set out on an excursion to Blenheim —the sculptor and myself being seated on the box of our four-horse carriage, two more of the party in the dicky, and others less agreeably accommodated inside. We had no coachman, but two postillions in short scarlet jackets and leather breeches with top-boots, each astride of a horse; so that all the way along, when not otherwise attracted, we had the interesting spectacle of their up-and-down bobbing in the saddle. It was a sunny and beautiful day, a specimen of the perfect English weather, just warm enough for comfort, yet retaining a mere spice or suspicion of austerity. . . . We saw one or two hamlets, and I especially remember a picturesque old gabled house at a turnpike-gate, and altogether the wayside scenery had an aspect of old-fashioned English life; but there was nothing very memorable till we reached Woodstock, and stopped to water our horses at the Black Bear. . . . The Black Bear is an ancient inn, large and respectable, with balustraded staircases, and intricate passages and corridors, and queer old pictures and engravings hanging in the entries and apartments. We ordered a lunch (the most delightful of English institutions, next to dinner) to be ready against our return, and then resumed our drive to Blenheim.

In a record of another journey, around East Anglia, he mentions the curious fact that at the station at Lincoln (and in 1855) there were no public cabs. There was only the hotel omnibus.

Another form of travel, neither road nor rail, in which Hawthorne found special delight, was river travel, which seems to have been new to him. In the record of a tour around Oxford, he describes a journey by sculler and by barge, and incidentally hands many compliments to the English climate and to English hospitality to the traveller. He called us "the kindest people on earth"; a case, I think, with Hawthorne, of finding what you bring. When they reached Oxford by sculler, they transferred to a barge:

> Here we took possession of a spacious barge, with a house in it and a comfortable dining-room or drawing-room within the house, and a level

roof on which we could sit at ease, or dance, if so inclined. These barges
are common at Oxford—some very splendid ones being owned by the
students of the different colleges, or by clubs. They are drawn by horses,
like canal-boats; and a horse being attached to our own barge, he trotted
off at a reasonable pace, and we slipped through the water behind him,
with a gentle and pleasant motion which was like no motion at all. . . .
In this happy state of mind and body we gazed at Christ Church meadows,
as we passed, and at the receding spires and towers of Oxford, and on
a good deal of pleasant variety along the banks: young men rowing or
fishing; troops of naked boys bathing, as if this were Arcadia, in the simplicity of the Golden Age; country houses, cottages, waterside inns, all
with something fresh about them, as not being sprinkled with the dust of
the highway. . . . Meanwhile a table had been laid in the interior of our
barge, and spread with cold ham, cold fowl, cold pigeon-pie, cold beef,
and other substantial cheer, such as the English love, and Yankees too—
besides tarts and cakes and pears and plums—not forgetting, of course, a
goodly provision of port, sherry, and champagne, and bitter ale, which is
like mother's milk to an Englishman, and soon grows equally acceptable
to his American cousin.

But for all ordinary purposes of travel, the railway, in almost all
parts, was conqueror. In that thoughtless phrase which people so
often used, and still use, the railway had "come to stay." They
said the same of the sedan-chair. They said the same of the coach.
They said the same of the horse-tram and the electric-tram. Yet a
brief glance at the history of man and his social appliances shows that
whatever he has invented has always been displaced by some new
invention. But in the middle nineteenth-century they were certain
that nothing could displace or even compete with the railway; and
they would have laughed if anyone had then told them that there
would come a time when the railways would be appealing for help
against the competition of road-travel and road-transport. What,
they would have asked, could possibly bring the dead road back to
life?

But those old coachmen in their lamentations were right about the
appeal of the road. In their own time they were proved wrong, but
in a long view they were right. The road was so essential a part of
the heritage of all of us, so much a part of the English mind and
spirit, that it could not pass from the English scene; it could not,
for very long, languish forgotten. The coachmen had no defence
against the challenge of the railway; yet they knew in their hearts,
though they could give no reason, that the life of the road would
return.

And it did. Very slowly at first, but surely. After fifty years of sleep, those roads which had twinkled and glittered for centuries with the legions and the pilgrims and the merchants, the woolpacks, the drovers, the horsemen, and the coaches, and then had lain still under the suns and frosts of many summers and winters; gradually they began to move to a thin trickle of travel. The bicycle began it. Then came that snorting, spluttering, ridiculed thing, the motor-car. They came at first as single pioneers, but soon the trickle became a little stream. Inns that had closed their doors, and become private houses, reopened for public use. Those that had given up receiving travellers, and had become only wayside beer-houses, looked to their beds, and hung out the white wings of the Cyclists' Touring Club. By the beginning of the twentieth century the road was fully awake again, and the inns were hanging out other signs—A.A., R.A.C., M.C.U. In the twentieth year of the twentieth century, the trickle had become a flood, and soon the roads were more dense with traffic than in even the Golden Age.

CHAPTER SIX

The Road Revives

THE CYCLE, as a mode of travel, was, like all innovations, at first hooted. It took a long time to gain favour, because, after it had survived the hooting, it came to be regarded as a public menace, and was detested. Cyclists "scorching" on the favourite cycling road, the London–Portsmouth road, were named Cads on Castors. That was before Mayfair and Belgravia took up cycling as a fashionable hobby, and went in hordes every morning to display themselves and their machines in—for some unearthly reason—Battersea Park.

The first cycles appeared on the road in 1869—the aptly named bone-shakers; and in eight or nine years cycling had become sufficiently general among those who couldn't afford horses, to warrant the publication of two weekly papers devoted to it, and the formation of two societies to watch the interests of cyclists. It was those societies that stirred up the authorities about the state of the roads, and went about the country fixing warning notice-boards—"To Cyclists. This Hill is Dangerous." After the bone-shaker (wooden wheels and iron tyres) came the high bicycle; the seat nearly five feet from the ground. This was called the Ordinary, and a special costume was worn with it: something between that of a District Messenger and a skating instructor. In the early 'eighties the Ordinary was displaced by the Safety, the type we know to-day, with rubber tyres. The tricycle was another model, but it had only a short career. It was considered too "elderly."

Cyclists, then, were the pioneers in the reopening of the roads. Indeed, they were almost road-makers. During the years of sleep, the roads had fallen into such decay that many, as I say, were in a seventeenth-century condition. It was by the vigorous agitation of the Cyclists' Touring Club and the Cyclists' Union that they were put into repair and made safe for travellers. Once they were in a fit state, there came a revival of road-life. Men began touring by dog-cart and gig and phaeton—see William Black's forgotten novel, *The Strange Adventures of a Phaeton*. There was a revival of amateur coaching, and in the 'seventies, many pleasure coaches (called "butterfly" coaches) were put on the road, running, during the summer months, from London to Windsor, Hampton Court, High Wycombe, Brighton, Tunbridge Wells, St. Albans, Guildford,

Maidenhead.   For the elderly, it revived memories of a past mode of travel, and for the younger it was a new sensation.

But the newest of sensations was cycling, and from a handbook on the pastime, published in 1873, it appears that it was a far more strenuous business than it is to-day.   You had at that time only a choice between the bone-shaker and the high bicycle, and you had to be pretty fit to do fifty miles on either.   So fit, that the handbook lays down rules to be followed in preparing for and making a long run.   Some of the rules read a little oddly to-day, notably in the allowance of alcohol.

The cold bath, early rising and early to bed, are the prime rules. Then you must in your meals avoid pork, veal, duck, salmon, and pastry.   You must feed on beef, mutton, fowl, and fish.   You must cut out bread, butter, milk, sugar, beer, and potatoes.   For breakfast you should take beef, mutton, kidneys, or bacon, with a cup of tea or coffee without milk.   For your midday meal, any fish except salmon, herrings or eels; any meat except that mentioned above; any vegetable except potato, parsnip, beetroot, turnip or carrot; any kind of poultry or game, and two or three glasses of good claret, sherry or Madeira.   No champagne or port or beer.   At tea-time, stewed fruit, a rusk or two, and tea without milk or sugar   For the evening meal, any of the allowed meats or fish already named, with a glass or two of claret or sherry.   On going to bed, a tumbler of grog —gin, whisky, or brandy, without sugar.   The tea-time rusk could be softened with a tablespoonful of gin or whisky.   It all sounds rather like training for a world lightweight championship, with a determination to lose, rather than preparation for a run such as the modern cyclist makes without noticing it.

The same handbook describes a cycle tour from London to the north, made by four members of a Cycling Club.   It is the earliest record of a cycle tour I have been able to find.   The party met at six in the morning, at the King's Arms Hotel, Kensington, and, after "a capital breakfast," they set out, escorted to the edge of London by more prudent members of the club, who there gave them God-speed on their foolhardy adventure.   They followed the Great North Road to Potter's Bar, where they made their first halt (one of many) for refreshment, and where the landlord gave them a cordial reception, and his daughter presented each of the quartet with "a flower." On to Welwyn, where they "halted for refreshments"; then through Stevenage to Baldock, where they dined, and rested for two hours. Then to Biggleswade, where they found a country fair in progress, and found themselves of greater interest than any of the side-shows.   A

83   "A World on Wheels, 1879"
From a "Punch" cartoon

84   The Bicycling Revival of Recent Days: a Roadside Scene

85 "Thomson's Road Steamer at Edinburgh," *ca.* 1870

86 A Steam Tram, *ca.* 1900

large crowd gathered to watch them oil their machines. Then on to Eaton Socon (halt for refreshments) and so to Buckden where they ran into so heavy a rainstorm that they put up for the night. They had covered 65 miles.

Next day they followed the road through Stilton, Norman Cross, and Wansford to Stamford. The road in that district was of limestone, and the rains had so washed them that they could hardly get along; the wheel-ruts being six inches deep and covering all the road. After "refreshments" at Stamford, they went on until they reached the hundredth milestone from London, when they dismounted and cheered, and had more "refreshment," this time from their pocket-flasks. Then on to Grantham, where they took a stroll round the town and found it "well worth seeing." Then on to Newark through another rainstorm, which drenched them. They stayed the night at Newark, and next day went on to Sutton-on-Trent. All through Rutland and Lincolnshire they noted the intense dislike shown to their machines by the horses, which in other counties had shown no disturbance.

From Sutton-on-Trent they went on through Tuxford to East Retford which they found "a very nice town, with several good hotels," which suggests that "refreshments" were double and treble. Then on to Scrooby, Bawtry, and so to Doncaster, where they had "a very good dinner." After dinner, they went on through Robin Hood's Well to Went Bridge, where they stayed the night at the Bay Horse. In the morning they were delayed by rain, but as at midday it showed no sign of stopping, they went on to Ferrybridge, where they "were compelled to remain at an hotel for the purpose of drying our clothes." When the clothes were dry, they remounted and went on to Abberford, and halted at the Swan "for refreshments." Then on to Wetherby, where they stayed the night, "spending a merry evening with a lot of jolly Yorkshiremen, the jovial song lending a charm to the entertainment."

At nine o'clock next morning they resumed their journey, and did a ten-mile run to Boroughbridge, where they took breakfast. After breakfast they made a run of twenty-five miles over an excellent road, but there was scarcely a house to be seen. They found no place where they could "halt for refreshments" until they reached Catterick Bridge, and the author advised intending travellers through Yorkshire to "provide themselves with everything needful beforehand." (Pocket-flask?) At Catterick Bridge they dined, and then went on to Darlington, where they put up. Next day they pedalled through Aycliffe to Durham, on good roads, and at the Half Moon they had "a capital dinner." And so to Newcastle, 277 miles in six days, with, so far as one can gather, no attention to the dietary laws laid down earlier.

In the late 'seventies James John Hissey began to make his first tours of England. His records of these tours are well known; he was publishing them from the early 'eighties to 1920. The first tours were made by various horse vehicles; the later by car. The titles of some of them indicate the mode he used: *On the Box Seat; A Drive Through England; Across England in a Dog Cart; A Tour in a Phaeton; An Old-Fashioned Journey*. Those done by car were: *The Road and the Inn; Untravelled England;* and one or two others. The earlier volumes are, of course, the more valuable, since they deal with a vanished England which only the very old ever saw. Hissey saw the road in its two phases; in its long slumber, and in its twentieth-century crowded life. On his early tours he came across many once-great inns with three-quarters of their rooms closed; on his later tours he often found trouble in getting accommodation. In the stables of some of those inns, in the 'seventies and 'eighties, he sometimes found relics of the Golden Age—crumbling post-chaises, mouldering drags, decayed coaches, strung with cobwebs.

He met few people on the roads, either main roads or byways, and expresses wonder that the inns they stayed at were able with so few travellers to keep open at all. Commercial representatives and angler were almost their only custom. For this reason, he found rather better treatment than he found in his motoring years. At all inns and farmhouses he and his party were cordially received; farmhouses often gave friendly refreshment to the travellers and their horses, and at several inns they were even presented, on leaving, with a bouquet from the garden and good wishes for the rest of the journey. He found that the farther an inn was from the railway, the better it was and the lower its charges. At many places they were the only guests, and were the first travellers that had been seen for some time. In those journeys of the 'seventies, he travelled with Paterson's *Roads*, an edition of 1829, and found it, so far as directions went, still accurate. The roads themselves, however, were not the same. In Yorkshire, Dorset, and Cornwall, he found some terrible roads. Bad weather and neglect had worked upon their surface, and he found them littered for miles with loose stones over which the phaeton rocked and jolted.

By the middle 'eighties conditions had much improved, and when the millionaire Carnegie made his coach tours, chiefly along main roads, he paid compliments to their excellent surface. Of one of

87   An old London Bus at work in Cornwall

88   Coal Barges on a Canal

89　Pioneers of Motoring

90　The Revival of the Four-in-Hand: a Scene in Hyde Park

those tours, from Brighton to Inverness, he wrote an account himself in *An American Four-in-Hand in Britain;* an account of another from Charing Cross to Ilfracombe, of which he was host, was written by one of his guests, under the title, *Chronicle of the Coach.* Two other guests on this occasion were William Black, the novelist, and Matthew Arnold. Carnegie, as a millionaire, travelled in the grand manner. Every stopping-place received advance notice of the arrival of his party, and at their inns and hotels a private drawing-room and dining-room were reserved for them. Neither of the tours therefore produced much incident of travel in the way of delightful surprises or mishaps.

This old eighteenth-century custom of dining in private was retained by many of the newer hotels of that time. They had no *table d'hôte* and no common lounge. The American traveller quoted in the previous chapter was a little querulous about this:

> Travellers must be allowed to talk and even grumble about hotels; for these are often the only "interiors" they see. . . . One is made exceedingly comfortable at a first-class English hotel, but there is a stiffness about it which is not apt to be found in the best American or Continental hotels. Seldom is there a public table; and if the party comprise ladies, one is forced, even if staying for a single day, to take a private parlor. But I am quite converted to the English private parlor. After a long day's journey in heat and dust, struggling on with an eager and vexed human current, to be ushered into one's own room, quiet as a room at home, furnished often with books and every luxury and comfort, this goes some way towards recompensing the traveller for the exclusiveness of the thing. He is, it is true, entirely isolated. If his dearest friend were dying in the next room, he would not find it out, for seldom is there a registry-book kept in an English hotel. And one rarely risks a question to the dignified and taciturn waiter, with gravity and white cravat enough to be the Dean of Westminster.

In a later passage, he reverts to the topic. He mentions the Englishman's suspicion of the stranger and the fear of giving himself away to an undesirable acquaintance. This suspicion, he says, meets one at the inn or hotel. The traveller is received coldly, and consigned to the care of Boots or the chambermaid. He is shut up alone in a parlour; is obliged to ring and ring for the most common services; and has to eat his dinner alone and in silence. The author had the idea that a traveller arriving at an hotel was looked upon as an intruder in a family circle. He was expected to keep his own room, to make as little noise as possible, and give as little trouble. Yet when he left, he was accosted by demands "from three or four understrappers to whom he was not aware of being indebted for any assistance."

Q*

At one point of his record he gives the prices charged by his hotel at Matlock—the New Bath Hotel, a first-class hotel. They read a little strangely in the eyes of us of to-day. Bedroom 2*s*. Breakfast 1*s*. 6*d*. Lunch 1*s*. to 2*s*. Dinner 2*s*. 6*d*. to 3*s*. Supper 1*s*. to 2*s*. Private room from 2*s*. 6*d*. to 5*s*. Full board 5*s*. 6*d*. a day. Sitting-room by the week 15*s*. Bedroom by the week—single 7*s*., double 14*s*. Maid's attendance per week on one person 7*s*.

On his country travels he encountered a type of Englishman whom he took the trouble to sketch—the commercial traveller:

> I was doomed to interminable conversations in railway carriages and coffee-rooms with hard-brained and plain-spoken men. I met among them oftentimes exceedingly well-informed individuals, and if one is a little cautious not to arouse national prejudices, there are few more interesting and graphic talkers than this class of person. They are men who blurt their thoughts out without fear or favour. They are practical men, who despise humbug and pipe-claying. They did not spare their national idols, their leading men. Even Gladstone, who was one of the best of them in their estimation, came in for his share; they called him "a bookman," who knew no more of finance than Boots here. They berated the boarding-houses of London, and in fact London tradespeople generally. This honest talk, if it sounds rough, lends an individuality and knotty picturesqueness to the commonest Englishman, and makes him stand out from the rest of mankind like a gnarled oak.

He appreciated our country food, and specially mentioned one or two local delicacies. He liked our ale and cider, and the Cornish "clouted cream," which he described as "a sort of superior bonny-clabber." One of his chapters took a leap into the future. He had not, he said, any special love of England, but he recognised that England and America were essentially one, with the same blood, faith, ideals and literature. Those things, he said, constituted a unit in nature and spirit that no external or accidental relations could ever create between America and other foreign nations, and:

> I have never lost sight of the principle that they should acknowledge this unity, that they *will* do so in the final struggle between free and despotic principles. Lord Derby has truly said that "no other earthly event would conduce so much to the future of civilisation as the union of these two countries."

Seventy years later, in the summer of 1941, the "final struggle between free and despotic principles" brought about that desired union.

The reopening of the road brought, in the late 'eighties and early 'nineties, a revival of interest in England itself. A new literature of the countryside appeared. Scores of people began to discover their own country and to write accounts of their tours. Publishers found that works on English Topography and English Travel sold as well as books on distant exploration. Macmillans launched their *Highways and Byways* series. Other publishers issued series of volumes on the counties—*Memorials of Old Middlesex* and other counties; and a series of *Picturesque Hertfordshire, Picturesque Essex*, etc. Charles G. Harper began his series of individual histories of the great

A Woman Bicyclist, 1897

roads, and of the old inns, and of the coasts. Among the large number of young people who went touring on foot, there was a huge sale for the series of *Field-Path Rambles*. The Thames valley became crowded with landscape painters. Cycling was taken up by poets and novelists. They went about in the new cycling costume of Norfolk jacket, knee-breeches, and woollen stockings. Women cyclists wore, not bloomers (they were never worn after the 'fifties), but Rational Dress—a jacket something like the man's Norfolk jacket wide breeches of the same material, black stockings and shoes, and a toque. Everybody was quoting Walt Whitman: "Afoot and light-hearted, I take to the open road. . . ."

In the middle of this revival of the road came the new thing. "Don't tell me, sir, that people will ever ride in those things. They'll never Do. What! When you can travel in comfort, is anybody likely to travel in those stinking, clattering things and get all smothered in dust and oil? Stink-pots—that's what they are—only fit for cads or lunatics." That was the kind of thing one heard in 1895. Just as the public had said that nobody would give up coaches for tea-kettle travel, so they said that the motor was Impossible, and would never Do. They would never be made to run properly; they would always be breaking down miles from anywhere. What use was a thing like that? It received the same treatment as the cycle—it was derided as useless and hooted as dangerous. In some cases, it was actually stoned, and the owners were attacked.

At first, of course, it did break down, five or six times in as many miles. It was always being pushed home or towed home. The diaries of the pioneer motorists are mainly records of breakdowns, with now and then a whoop of triumph at the achievement of a twenty-mile journey without a single mishap. Those motorists spent much of their time on their backs underneath the engine. A diary of 1895, quoted in the Badminton volume on *Motoring*, published in 1902, is a string of misadventures. When the car was delivered, the owner tried to start it with the starting-handle. He began in the afternoon, and by the time darkness came nothing had resulted except a pair of worn-out gloves. Next day he tried some new oil, and the dealer gave him naphtha, which mucked up the car for a week. Then he got some benzoline, and the car began to go. At a small town near Portsmouth he was followed by a hooting crowd, and had to beat them off with umbrellas. The police took name and address. He was summoned and fined for using a horseless carriage without a man on foot in front of it, with a red flag. A week later he frightened a horse drawing a milk-cart, and the cans went clattering all over the street. Other entries record nuts lost from different screws; carburet-tor tube choked; an involuntary swerve into the kerbstone, which smashed the frame; accumulators giving out; the blowing-out of the asbestos joint of the exhaust-box; and so on; ending with the pushing of the car into a stable, and taking a cab.

The first petrol-driven car ever seen in England was introduced by the Hon. Evelyn Ellis in 1895. In defiance of the law concerning a herald with a red flag, he drove across England without one, and though the police saw him, no prosecution was brought against him. Others followed his example in flouting an antiquated law, and in 1896 the law was revoked, and the motoring boom began. As with the cycle, so with the car; almost at once periodicals devoted to the automobile began to appear. The *Autocar* made its first appearance in 1895; the *Automotor* in 1896.

It is a curious fact that all our modes of conveyance have been imported from abroad. The first coach seen in England—that given to Elizabeth—came from abroad. The sedan-chair came from abroad.

91 King George V in the first Rolls-Royce, 1905

92 The Rolls-Royce of 1938

93 Buses on London Bridge: a recent photograph

So did the cabriolet, the omnibus, and the velocipede and the auto-mobile. The first cars seen here were either French or German. Their names indicate their origin—Benz, Darracq, De Dion, Panhard, Mercedes, Serpollet, Daimler, Lutzmann, Peugeot, Renault. Some of them were steam-cars, some electric, and some "petroleum-driven." Lord Northcliffe (then Alfred Harmsworth) was one of the most prominent supporters of the new thing, as he was, later, of the aeroplane; and he was one of the earliest motorists. At the end of the century he owned a fleet of cars—four French, two American, two English, and several others. In the late 'nineties he took W. E. Henley for a run in one of those cars—a run which produced the first poetic celebration of the new thing—*A Song of Speed*.

The car "took" with the public almost as quickly as the railway. Companies for its manufacture came with a rush, though many years passed before any but the well-to-do could possess one. At the beginning of the century, the cheapest car was about £250, and the cost of upkeep was much heavier than it is to-day. Most of them were of the open tourer sort, and therefore a special costume was necessary. Goggles, fitted to the head with leather straps, were worn by all the earlier motorists. Women wore not only goggles, but thick veils which went over the hat. They wore coats of chamois or opos-sum, and the men wore leather coats or Robinson Crusoe coats of goat-skin, with leather gloves. They looked indeed pretty much like the aeroplane pilots of to-day.

It is in the nature of things that the inns, which were to benefit so largely from the new travel, were at first hostile to it. Most of them were hostile to cyclists until they saw the custom that flowed to two inns that welcomed cyclists—the Anchor and the Talbot, at Ripley. The first inn that welcomed the motorist, and turned its old stabling into garages, was an inn on the Brighton Road. Its owner was laughed at. But not for long. Other innkeepers saw that there might, after all, be something in this motoring craze. People might really take up those stinking things. Already a number of wealthy people had them, and might bring profitable custom. So they discarded their hostility, and had a look at their stabling. In the early days of cycling, those few inns that did not despise the cyclist hung out notices—"Accommodation for Cyclists"; though why they should have been "accommodated" is one of the mysteries of that bastard language called Commercial English. In the same way, those inns that were ready to welcome the motorist, in the days before the word "garage" was in use, hung out notices—"Stabling for Motor Cars. Engineer in Attendance." "Chauffeur" had not then been introduced. Car-owners called their driver "the engineer."

In the days before A.A. scouts and patrols, boys of the villages and towns would hang about on the outskirts, waiting for a chance, which often came, of earning a sixpence. Whenever a car broke down there always appeared, out of the earth as it were, a group of boys who stood and stared at it until the expected inquiry came—"Will you lads help me push it into the village?" One of the trials of the early motorist was the number of people—not only lads willing to help—who gathered round him or her in a breakdown, and stared and giggled, or hummed the popular song of the day:

> Oh, Flo, why did you go
> Riding alone in your motor-car?
> Some people say you are singular,
> Peculiar, and so you are. . . .

Pioneers, O Pioneers! They have always had a raw deal, and always from the very people who were later to enjoy the results of their trials and troubles. Common—very common—injunctions to the stranded motorist were, "Whip be'ind, guv'nor," or, "Put 'is nose-bag on; p'r'aps he'll go then," or, "Try getting 'im out of the shafts. He's only got the windy staggers." But those early motorists were imperturbable. They knew they had "got something," and they were fascinated, even dazed by it. They lived for their cars, and suffered for them, and sat up at nights with them, tinkering and tinkering. The car was much more than a new toy; it was a chariot leading to a new way of life and new horizons. The people might jeer as they pleased; the motorist took no more notice of them than a man in love.

Within the first decade of this century, the car established itself not only as a private conveyance, but for public transport in the form of motor-bus, motor-lorry, and motor char-à-banc. In eighty years the means of travel had passed from the age of the horse, through the age of steam, to the age in which we still live—the age of petrol. Within a further ten years the cheap car for Everyman arrived, and the English roads saw many novel features added to the familiar features of travel. Every mile of main and secondary roads was traversed. At every few miles signs were set up in the form of circles, triangles, diamonds, giving various warnings. Telephone-boxes appeared in lonely valleys and on remote hills. At cross-roads on the main highways were scouts in uniforms of blue or drab. Signposts multiplied. They were set up at almost every lane and by-way. Old milestones were repainted, and new mileage indicators, with bold figures, were erected at important points. The old custom of ambush was revived. Behind hedges, and in woods by the roadside, men lay in wait for the traveller—not with intent of robbery or physical violence; only with intent of catching offenders against the speed-limit. The English appetite for tea seemed to increase tenfold, if the supply represented the demand. In every village, in every hamlet of the most rural and secluded corners, in the gardens of isolated roadside cottages, appeared the notice—*Teas and Minerals*—usually handwritten, and with the "s" reversed.

Those people who could not afford cars of their own were able none the less to do their long-distance travelling by road, in the manner of their great-grandfathers. The luxurious, long-distance motor-coach arrived, complete with coffee and sandwich buffet. They could go to the London coach office, in the manner of great-grandfather, and book their places on the night coach for Manchester and Glasgow, Newcastle and Edinburgh, or the day coaches for Birmingham or Bristol or Exeter. The road was now awake through daylight and dark. Death on the road was frequent, but adventures on the road were few. Asphalt and tarmac covered the surfaces of Macadam and Telford, and speed gave little opportunity for casual encounter or highway hold-ups. In any trouble, or perplexity about route, there was always a scout or patrol to put the traveller right.

Within another ten years the roads became so crowded, speed was so high, drivers so reckless, and deaths so many, that at cross-roads on the highway, obstacles, in the form of a green circular enclosure, were set at the middle of the road to compel drivers to check their speed. On roads where straight, flat stretches enable a driver to hold a high speed over two or three miles—as on parts of the Exeter road and Birmingham road—these roundabouts are useful. Other new features were the arterial roads cut in a direct line from point to point; the by-passes which avoided the bottle-neck roads of towns and villages; and the rounding of corners whose trees or bushes concealed a side-road.

Under the inspiration of this ceaseless flow of traffic, not only did the old inns move with the times by redecorating themselves and modernising their amenities; new inns were opened, with a new kind of innkeeper. Also, a new kind of place, not exactly inn or hotel, appeared. Private houses and cottages on the main roads were taken, and opened as Guest Houses, or as places for light lunches and teas in a well-kept garden, where the tables were fitted with brilliantly coloured sunshades. Most of these places were unlicensed. Another

R

development was that some of the large country houses were taken over and opened as country clubs. With so much road transport by night as well as day another new thing appeared—the lorry-drivers' hotel and snack-bar and roadside caravanserai. Then, in the roaring 1920's, came the Road-house on the American model, with palm lounge, ball-room, dance-band, swimming-pool, cocktail bar, grill-room, and "fruit" machines. At all these new places light meals could be had at any time, which is not the rule at the ordinary hotel or inn.

The new innkeepers who took over some of the older inns reverted to a type of about a hundred years earlier. They were intelligent and cultivated men; sometimes men who had followed one of the professions; and they had studied the business of innkeeping and had seen where it might be improved. Those new men paid special attention to something that the majority of inns leave to routine treatment—the kitchen and the cellar. They introduced careful cooking and new dishes. Their wine-lists were as serious as those of the best London restaurants. Their furniture harmonised with the period of their particular inn or hotel. They made acquaintance with each guest, instead of leaving him to come and go as a cypher.

The Trust House Company also took a great part in the inn's new life. It bought up decayed inns, restored them where they needed restoring (but always in the spirit of their original) and put them into the modern procession. Where it found beautiful features, it retained them and worked round them. It made a special point of combining ancient architectural grace with modern service and cheerful decoration. The motorists' associations also did their share in reawakening the inn generally, showing its keepers what the modern traveller required, and holding them to a certain standard.

While all this crowded road-travel was going on, a new form of travel was developing. By 1910 the air had been conquered. The thing was, of course, at first frowned upon. To some people the exploration and exploitation of the air seemed a wickedness. Their common remark was—"If we'd been meant to fly, we'd have been given wings." The pioneers made their own wings. In 1911, the airman Beaumont made a circuit of Great Britain, 1,010 miles, in twenty-two hours. Before the last war, mails were being carried by plane, and in the 'twenties came the passenger-carrying plane. Air travel across England became general. As the railways had outdone the coaches in the matter of time, so did the plane outdo the railway. Those first passengers discovered a new England; so new that archaeologists began to make use of air-travel. From above they could locate lost tracks, the sites of early British or Roman encampments which numbers of people had walked over without perceiving, and old barrows and earthworks. London business men doing business with Manchester, Leeds, or Glasgow, found that they could save hours in making the journey by air; though what business men do with the time they "save" I have never discovered. Do they bank it? Whatever they do with it, they seemed glad to save it, and up to the outbreak of this war, air-travel was well used across England. Flying clubs were being developed, and numbers of people owned private planes.

Everybody was travelling, either by air, by rail, or by road or footpath. Families went touring in the family car. There were tours by motor-coach—two or three days—at an inclusive charge for fare and hotel. The railways took a part in the See-England-First enthusiasm, and published lavishly illustrated holiday books describing the resorts on their particular line. They issued tourist tickets entitling the holder to stop off at any places he chose in a given district. Books on English tours and English topography multiplied, and the motoring associations and the Travel and Industrial Development Association published outline tours of specific interest—as cathedrals, castles, old towns, etc.—with routes.

At week-ends the countryside was dotted with walkers, some alone, some in groups. In the lanes and by-ways the ice-cream tricycle—Stop Me and Buy One—catered for their casual refreshment. For their service in other ways a new association was formed. It was the Youth Hostels Association, and it set up across England a string of hostels for hard-up walkers; some of them new buildings and some of them gracious old manor-houses, and all of them in pleasant country surroundings and within one day's walk of each other. For an entrance fee of five shillings, members could have the use of them for one shilling a night. They could either cook their own food in the kitchen, or buy supper and breakfast from the Warden. In the morning, since the only staff was the Warden, they did their own washing-up and made their own beds, and did any tidying that might be necessary so that the place was left clean and neat for the new arrivals in the evening.

Up to the beginning of the war, all sorts of young people, and some not so young, met in the hostels: factory workers, clerks, undergraduates, schoolmasters, young artists, and young people from Europe; and the evenings were filled with bright discussion. At the time of writing they are not, of course, so much in use as they were;

some of them are in areas where travelling is suspended. But quite a number are still doing useful work in providing cheap centres for war-workers on holiday, and after the war, so useful a service to so large a number of young people is certain to be extended.

Travel during the war was mainly limited to travel of urgent need. Travel for pleasure, except at holiday times, for the workers and men of the forces who earned a break, was rightly little indulged in. Also, many coast resorts, at the time of writing, could not be visited, and many hotels and large inns in other parts of the country were being used for other purposes. But the travel of urgent need brought strange life to the roads, and moving scenes. Vehicles of all sorts, were brought into use. Day and night the roads hummed and throbbed more than at any other time in their history. And the railways and every other mode of movement were used to their limit.

Meantime, those who loved touring had put the car in dock, and, after work, supplied the lack of real wandering by reading some of the many books of the past describing journeys and wanderings along the roads and across the fields of England. Those wanderings, as this book shows, have followed many modes. Whether any new mode will arise in the future, I cannot, lacking the prescience of H. G. Wells, conjecture. Men have travelled the road on foot, on horseback, by coach, by steam, by petrol. They have travelled by electricity under the earth and under the beds of rivers. They have travelled in the air. Is any new mode possible? And will it be faster and faster? Or will men be content, not to get from place to place in forty seconds, but to recover the joy of somehow, in the course of twelve-month, getting to Birmingham by way of Beachy Head?

Index

(The numerals in italics denote the *figure numbers of* illustrations)

151